Celebrating your year
1971
a very special year for

A message from the author:

Welcome to the year 1971.

I trust you will enjoy this fascinating romp down memory lane.

And when you have reached the end of the book, please join me in the battle against AI generated copy-cat books and fake reviews.

Details are near the back of the book.

Best regards,
Bernard Bradforsand-Tyler.

Contents

1971 Family Life in the USA 8
Life in the United Kingdom 12
Hippies and the Rise of the Communes . 16
Tuning in to Television 19
Our Love Affair with Automobiles 23
Clean Air for All 28
Greenpeace Takes to the Seas 30
Nuclear Bomb Testing 31
Anti-Vietnam War Sentiment 33
Pentagon Papers White House Scandal . 34
Space Missions of 1971 36
Troubles in Northern Ireland 40
   Bangladesh War of Independence 42
   Death Sentence for Charles Manson 44
   Walt Disney World Opens 46
Jesus Christ Superstar on Broadway 47
1971 in Cinema and Film 48
Top Grossing Films of the Year 49
A Decade of Disasters 50
   Musical Memories 52
   1971 Billboard Top 30 Songs 54
   Fashion Trends of the 1970s 58
   Also in Sports 65
Invention of the Electronic Mail 67
Other News from 1971 68
Famous People Born in 1971 72
1971 in Numbers 76
Image Attributions 84

Advertisement

Instead of giving your teenager another sermon on sloppy handwriting, give him a Smith-Corona.

He's probably heard enough sermons to recite them by heart.

And has it done any good?

If not, perhaps it's time you tried something else. Perhaps it's time for a Smith-Corona. Like our electric portable.

With it, your teenager can learn to type twice as fast as writing by hand.

His spelling can improve because a typed word that's misspelled just begs to be corrected.

Thinking gets a nudge, too, because a typewriter can accept ideas as fast as they appear.

And then a quiet little miracle called Organization occurs. When that happens, pride, confidence and self-esteem can start to show themselves.

It's smooth sailing from there.

But why Smith-Corona?

Because all typewriters are not the same. That's why we invite you to compare a Smith-Corona against any other typewriter.

Compare durability. Portability. Features.

Compare years of experience in manufacturing (especially electric portables).

When you do, you'll know why more people in the world buy Smith-Corona Electric Portables than any other.

And why you should, too.

You'll find our dealers in the Yellow Pages.

SMITH-CORONA

**We think we make better students.
We know we make better typewriters.**

He's probably heard enough sermons to recite them by heart. And has it done any good? If not, perhaps it's time you tried something else. Perhaps it's time for a Smith-Corona. Like our electric portable. With it, your teenager can learn to type twice as fast as writing by hand. His spelling can improve because a typed word that's misspelled just begs to be corrected. Thinking gets a nudge, too, because a typewriter can accept ideas as fast as they appear. And then a quiet little miracle called Organization occurs. When that happens, pride, confidence and self-esteem can start to show themselves. It's smooth sailing from there.

But why Smith-Corona?

Because all typewriters are not the same. That's why we invite you to compare a Smith-Corona against any other typewriter. Compare durability. Portability. Features. Compare years of experience in manufacturing (especially electric portables). When you do, you'll know why more people in the world buy Smith-Corona Electric Portables than any other. And why you should, too. You'll find our dealers in the Yellow Pages.

We think we make better students.   We know we make better typewriters.

Let's flashback to 1971, a very special year.

Was this the year you were born?

Was this the year you were married?

Whatever the reason, this book is a celebration of your year,

THE YEAR 1971.

Turn the pages to discover a book packed with fun-filled fabulous facts. We look at the people, the places, the politics and the pleasures that made 1971 unique and helped shape the world we know today.

So get your time-travel suit on, and enjoy this trip down memory lane, to rediscover what life was like, back in the year 1971.

1971 Family Life in the USA

Imagine if time-travel was a reality, and one fine morning you wake up to find yourself flashed back in time, back to the year 1971.

What would life be like for a typical family, in a typical town, somewhere in America?

Young people at a May Day concert, 1st May 1971.

In the early '70s our cultural gaze had shifted away from London's Swinging Sixties, back to the USA. The hippie view of the world, with its emphasis on peace, love and nature, focused our collective attention on the anti-war and anti-pollution movements.

We were fed-up with the ongoing Cold War and the draining war in Vietnam. We were ready for a new focus and a new vision. The counterculture movements of the late '60s continued well into the 1970s, as we rejected the old traditions and conservative values of our parents. Women, African Americans, LGBT communities and environmentalists would ramp up the fight for recognition and equality.

In the ten years to 1971, the US population had increased by 11.5% to 211.4 million.[1] The first of the Baby Boomers were now a vocal population of young adults. Birth rates and family sizes were falling, thanks to changing family values and readily available contraceptives.

1971 May Day protest, Washington D.C.

Women's Strike for Equality march, 26th Aug 1970, New York, USA.

At the same time, divorce rates were rising. The feminist movement had left women more educated and confident. As no-fault divorce laws came into effect, couples could legally divorce for any or no reason at all. An estimated 50% of couples who married in 1971 would end up divorced in future years.[2]

Levels of education had also increased—80% of 17-year-olds graduated high school in 1971 (up from 69.5% ten years earlier).[3] A further 36% of 18 to 19-year-olds continued to a higher education institution.[4]

[1] worldometers.info/world-population.
[2] nationalaffairs.com/publications/detail/the-evolution-of-divorce.
[3] usafacts.org/data/topics/people-society/education.
[4] statista.com/statistics/236093/higher-education-enrollment-rates-by-age-group-us.

The picture is brighter in America's parking lots.

Driving up to a Fotomat store is just about the easiest way in the whole world to get a roll of pictures developed.

Plus your pictures themselves will probably look better.

We're the country's largest retailer of photographic services. With over 1,000 drive-through stores in parking lots coast-to-coast. With a few exceptions.

Such as the Fotomat store that opened with "six flags over mid-America" this summer in St. Louis. It's a living history book built over 200 magnificently landscaped acres. There are rides like the famous Log Flume, and shows for everyone in the family—and we're inside the gates.

We want to make picture-taking easier. Anywhere we are.

Did you know that the term "generation gap" was coined by the Baby Boomers to describe the differences between their attitudes and values, and those of their old-world parents? This new generation questioned everything about "the American Dream", even mixing their social and political views into their music and art.

A family portrait, 1970.

Universities and colleges became breeding grounds for free-thinking, liberal theories. Students often shared accommodation, partly for convenience and cost savings, but also as an expression of a new way of living, cohabiting, exploring sexual freedoms and spiritual fulfillment.

College students on campus, 1971.

In 1971 the median family income was $10,290 a year.[1] Unemployment stood at 6%, with GDP growth at 3.3%.[2]

Average costs in 1971 [3]	
New house	$26,216
New car	$3,600
Dishwasher	$180
Gallon of gasoline	$0.36

[1] census.gov/library/publications/1972/demo/p60-85.html.
[2] thebalance.com/unemployment-rate-by-year-3305506.
[3] thepeoplehistory.com and mclib.info/reference/local-history-genealogy/historic-prices/.

Life in the United Kingdom

Now just imagine you flashed back to a town in 1971 England. Although not all doom and gloom, the United Kingdom had found itself slipping on the world stage as America and the USSR battled for domination.

London had reigned as the center of global culture during the decade of the '60s, but by the '70s the shine had mostly faded. The joyful, care-free optimism of England's Swinging Sixties could not last forever.

London street scenes from the early '70s.

The sentiment on the streets had shifted from frivolity to revolution. This attitude was echoed in the fashion, music, art and culture of the time.
The "Troubles" in Northern Ireland affected the mood of the Nation. Nationalist campaigns had become increasingly violent, spilling into the streets of cities across the UK as activists took to bombing commercial and political targets.

The British feminist movement had a long-established history and continued to gain strength throughout the 1970s.

In March 1971, 4,000 women took to the streets for the first march of the newly formed Women's Liberation Movement. Their list of equal rights demands included equal education, equal pay, and free contraception.

The first Women's Liberation Movement protest march, 8th March 1971.

In 1971 the average age of marriage for women was 25, and the average age for the birth of their first child was 27.[1] The fertility rate was 2.2 births per woman, down from a peak of 2.9 in 1964.[2] The contraceptive pill (available since 1961) and the legalisation of abortion in 1967 aided in this decline.

The Divorce Reform Act came into effect in January 1971, allowing for divorce without reason and leading to a steep increase in divorce rates.

In the early '70s less than 50% of families owned a car.[3] Within the larger cities, most people still relied on public transport.

10% of homes did not have internal toilets, while 9% were still without baths.

58% lacked telephones and 66% lacked central heating.[4]

Only 33% of 18-year-olds finished high school, a figure far lower than most other industrialized nations.

[1&2] ons.gov.uk/peoplepopulationandcommunity.
[3&4] ons.gov.uk/ons/rel/ghs/general-lifestyle-survey/2011/rpt-40-years.html

Advertisement

ENCYCLOPAEDIA BRITANNICA
and introducing
Britannica's PRE-SCHOOL Library
included
FREE

Plus Britannica Junior FREE of extra cost

Give your child a head start now with Britannica's Pre-School Library. Each book covers basic and important childhood experiences – with words, numbers, colors, sounds, shapes, sizes, time, measures, nature and many other things. 13 volumes, beautifully illustrated, entirely in full color with read-aloud passages to help your child discover the world about him.

You get all volumes now... pay later on easy Book a Month Payment Plan.

Yes, the latest edition of Britannica – the greatest treasury of knowledge ever published – is now available on a remarkable Cooperative Offer. Under the terms of this truly amazing offer, you may obtain the latest edition of Britannica Junior at no extra cost when you choose Encyclopaedia Britannica. Also included, *free*, the new Britannica Pre-School Library–*First Adventures in Learning*. The 3 complete sets will be placed in your home NOW. You pay *later* on convenient budget terms. *Easy as buying a book a month.*

The Britannica Pre-School Library–*First Adventures in Learning*–is now available from Britannica. It represents years of editorial and educational experience and was designed to provide every child with better pre-school preparation. This Pre-School Library offers a wealth of exciting new materials which acquaint the smaller child with the world in which he lives through simple words, pictures, and signs.

Britannica Junior is a big, 15-volume set written, illustrated and indexed especially for children in grade school and junior high. Carefully matched to school subjects as a homework reference, it's rich in picture interest, and is easy to read and understand. And it leads right into Encyclopaedia Britannica.

Encyclopaedia Britannica Offers Thousands of Subjects of Practical Value. The new edition of Britannica has special articles on household budgets, interior decorating, medicine, health, home remodeling, child care and much more... useful information that can save you many dollars.

New Edition is Profusely Illustrated. The new Encyclopaedia Britannica offers over 22,000 magnificent illustrations—thousands in vivid color. But it does not merely show "attractive pictures"—it is the work of 10,400 of the world's great authorities.

Essential for Homework. For students, Britannica is indispensable. It is the finest, most complete reference published in America. It helps develop the active, alert minds that bring success in school and later life.

May we send you, free and without obligation, our new Preview Booklet which pictures and describes the latest edition of Encyclopaedia Britannica? We'll also include details on how you can receive Britannica's Pre-School Library and Britannica Junior Encyclopaedia–free of extra cost on our Cooperative Plan. Just mail the attached postage-free card today.

FREE!
Mail card now for Special New **Preview Booklet**
and complete details on this remarkable offer.

You get all volumes now... pay later on easy Book a Month Payment Plan.

Yes, the latest edition of Britannica–the greatest treasury of knowledge ever published–is now available on a remarkable Cooperative Offer. Under the terms of this amazing offer, you may obtain the latest edition of Britannica Junior *at no extra cost* when you choose Encyclopaedia Britannica. Also included, *free*, the Britannica Pre-School Library–*First Adventures in Learning*. The 3 complete sets will be placed in your home NOW. You pay *later* on convenient budget terms. *Easy as buying a book a month.*

The Britannica Pre-School Library–*First Adventures in Learning*–is now available from Britannica. It represents years of editorial and educational experience and was designed to provide every child with better pre-school preparation. This Pre-School Library offers a wealth of exciting new materials which acquaint the smaller child with the world in which he lives through simple words, pictures, and signs.

Britannica Junior is a big, 15-volume set written, illustrated, and indexed especially for children in grade school and junior high. Carefully matched to school subjects as a homework reference, it's rich in picture interest, and is easy to read and understand. And it leads right into encyclopaedia Britannica.

Encyclopaedia Britannica Offers Thousands of Subjects of Practical Value. The new edition of Britannica has special articles on household budgets, interior decorating, medicine, health, home remodeling, child care and much more...useful information that can save you many dollars.

Essential for Homework. For students, Britannica is indispensable. It is the finest, most complete reference published in America. It helps develop the active, alert minds that bring success in school and later life.

At midnight on 15th February 1971, after years of planning, the UK switched to the new decimal currency.

Posters for the new decimal system were displayed everywhere.

By 1971 the UK was nearly half-way through repaying its post-war debt to America and Canada. The 20-year post-war building boom, which had kept cash flowing and unemployment low, was over.

Economic growth in the UK was only half that of Germany and Japan, with annual GDP having slipped from 2nd place in 1960 (behind only USA), to 5th place in 1971. Moreover, UK GDP per capita had slipped to 24th place in world rankings.[1]

Industrial Relations Bill protest, 1st March 1971.

By 1971, most of the former colonies of the United Kingdom had been granted independence. The cost for the UK to keep and defend them had proven too heavy a burden.

Industrial strife was high, and inflation was on the rise. The UK in 1971 was a country in decline. And this was just the beginning. The worse was yet to come.

The remainder of the decade would bring a mounting series of economic crises, industrial actions and major political battles.

Engineering workers' strike at Tower Hill, London, 1st March 1973.

[1] nationmaster.com/country-info/stats/Economy/GDP.

Hippies and the Rise of the Communes   1960s—1970s

By the early '70s, the Baby Boomers were young adults. Everything about them was a break-away from their parents: their music, their fashion, their values, their personal and sexual freedoms. They were non-traditional, non-conformists, anti-authority, anti-consumerist, anti-war, politically active, experimental drug users, hippies, believers and disbelievers. Anything was possible. Everything was acceptable.

The "Back to the Land" movement and the rise of communal living in the late '60s and early '70s were lifestyle expressions of freedom of choice. Communes were anti-establishment and experimental, communes were whatever the inhabitants chose them to be. Up to 3000 communes existed in the USA during this period.[1]

In the state of Vermont, a haven for hippies, an estimated one third of young adults (below age 34) were living communally.[2]

[1&2] forbes.com/sites/russellflannery/2021/04/11/what-happened-to-americas-communes/?sh=7454bc05c577

Most communes encouraged co-ownership of possessions, collective chores and shared child-raising. For many, clothes, monogamy and drug usage were optional. By rejecting the 40-hour work week, many communards relied on food stamps, or temporary odd jobs to keep themselves nourished.

In rural areas communards practiced living off the land, setting up farms, building their own houses and selling handicrafts.

Myrtle Hill Farm, Vermont.

A geodesic dome house built at Myrtle Hill Farm, Vermont. Recalls one communard, "In 1971 a young man named Bernie Sanders visited Myrtle Hill Farm... Sanders' tendency to just sit around talking politics and avoid actual physical labor got him the boot."[1]

Communards at Hog Farm, California.

The rise of communal living in the late '60s and early '70s was worldwide. Although the vast majority only survived a few years, some communes continue to exist today.

[1] From *We Are As Gods: Back to the Land in the 1970s on the Quest for a New America* by Brian Doherty.

Advertisement

This year's sale is special because it includes over 75 of the best 1971 color TV and stereo sets we make.
  Not just a few leftover models.
  This year's color TVs are special because they have the sharpest big screen picture tube ever made. Some even have our new instant pushbutton tuner, and 100% solid-state Gibraltar chassis.
  This year's console stereos are special because they all have air suspension speakers. Precision turntables. Powerful amplifiers. And sensitive AM/FM tuners.
  The portable stereos are special because they're inexpensive to begin with.
  So if you want something very special—and you want to save a lot of money—drop in to your nearest Sylvania dealer.
  But do it now. Remember, some sales really do end.

Tuning in to Television

The television was our must-have appliance of the mid-20th century, taking pride of place in our family or living rooms. By 1971, 95.5% of US households owned a television.[1]

Color TVs had been around since the early '50s, however very few people purchased them. Broadcasting in color did not take off until 1965. Within two years, all the networks broadcast in color. By 1971, an estimated 48% of American households owned a color TV.[2]

Although some countries, like Canada and the UK, were catching up to the US with color TV broadcasting and ownership, Australia would wait till 1975 for its first color television broadcasts.

Elsewhere in the world, rates of television ownership lagged behind the USA.

In many countries, television networks were government owned or subsidized, allowing for more focus on serious documentaries and news, without the constant concern of generating advertising revenue.

Carroll O'Connor and Mike Evans in *All in the Family* (CBS. 1971-1979).

Most Popular TV Shows of 1971 [3]

1	All in the Family	=	Here's Lucy
2	The Flip Wilson Show	12	Hawaii Five-O
3	Marcus Welby, M.D.	13	Medical Center
4	Gunsmoke	14	The NBC Mystery Movie
5	ABC Movie of the Week	15	Ironside
6	Sanford and Son	16	The Partridge Family
7	Mannix	17	The F.B.I.
8	Funny Face	18	The New Dick Van Dyke Show
=	Adam-12	19	The Wonderful World of Disney
10	The Mary Tyler Moore Show	20	Bonanza

[1] americancentury.omeka.wlu.edu/items/show/136.
[2] tvobscurities.com/articles/color60s/.
[3] Nielsen Media Research 1971-'72 season of top-rated primetime television series in the USA.

Although sitcoms and variety programs remained popular in 1971, a new wave of intense TV dramas was keeping us glued to our television sets. A slew of police, detective, or medical themed primetime TV programs hit our screens in the late '60s, and we were hooked.

Eight of the twenty top-ranking TV series for 1971 were medical or crime themed programs, most lasting well into the decade.

Zulu, Jack Lord, James MacArthur and Kam Fong in *Hawaii Five-O* (CBS. 1968-1980).

Airing for an impressive 12 seasons, *Hawaii Five-O* was largely shot on location in Honolulu, Hawaii. It followed a special police task force fighting organized crime across the Hawaiian Islands.

The original series ended in 1980. A 2010 remake, based on the original series, ran for ten seasons.

Robert Young as Marcus Welby, with James Brolin as his head-strong young assistant and Elena Verdugo as their nurse, in *Marcus Welby, M.D.* (ABC. 1969-1976).

The Sonny & Cher Comedy Hour (CBS. 1971-1974).

Dick Van Dyke, Hope Lange, Angela Powell & Michael Shea in *The New Dick Van Dyke Show* (CBS. 1971-1974).

The television networks were quick to turn out new programs to keep us tuning in. Here are a few of the new programs that aired for the first time in 1971: *All in the Family, The Sonny & Cher Comedy Hour, The New Dick Van Dyke Show, Columbo,* and *The Jackson 5ive* Other notables include *The Two Ronnies*, and *Parkinson* (both BBC1, UK).

Peter Falk in *Columbo* (NBC. 1971-1978).

Ronnie Barker and Ronnie Corbett in *The Two Ronnies* (BBC1. 1971-1987).

Advertisement

We want to introduce as many people as possible to the finest-designed, best-built Chryslers we've ever offered. So we're coming through with the Royal. A brand-new series of Chryslers. At a new low price. $112 less than any other Chrysler series.
   Royal is every inch a Chrysler. Uncompromisingly full-sized.
   Royal is just as big as our most expensive New Yorker.
   It's also a bigger car than our chief competition, Buick LeSabre and Olds Delta 88.
   With a roomier interior. And a bigger trunk.
   Even the engine is bigger.
   Royal also comes with a torsion-bar suspension system. LeSabre and Delta use coil springs.
   Which is better?
   Well, it's interesting to note that GM does use torsion bars on two models; one of the most expensive Cadillacs, and the most expensive Oldsmobile.
   Now are we coming through?
   Royal. An introduction to what a full-sized car should be.
   A Chrysler. At a price you can afford.

Our Love Affair with Automobiles

Our love affair with automobiles began back in the early '50s, and by 1971 America's car addiction was unrivalled in the world. More than 92 million cars traveled our roads. Automobile numbers had risen 46% during the preceding 10 years. Although car costs had risen markedly, so too had real wages, making them increasingly affordable. The family car had become a necessity we could not survive without.

Americans purchased 10.24 million cars in 1971, setting a new record.

Traffic congestion in Boston, 1971.

Increased car ownership and the creation of the National Highway System gave us a new sense of freedom. Office commuters could live further out from city centers, in cleaner and more spacious suburban developments, and commute quickly and comfortably to work.

Rural areas faced a steady decline as the suburban population continued to rise. By the early 1970s, only 26% of the population remained in rural areas.

SouthPark Mall in Charlotte, North Carolina, 1971.

Catering to the suburban lifestyle, fully enclosed, air-conditioned shopping malls sprang up country-wide. A typical design saw one or two anchor stores with hundreds of smaller specialty shops sitting within a vast expanse of carparks.

DEMON 340
...the performance is a lot more than painted on.

Detroit was the car manufacturing powerhouse of America, where "the Big Three" (Ford, General Motors and Chrysler) produced the bulk of cars sold. Although still renowned for their gas-guzzling "muscle cars", pressure from imports and demand for more compact, fuel-efficient cars, led to a general downsizing. Compact and sub-compact car sales grew, increasing markedly after the Arab embargo oil crisis of 1973.

1971 was the year American muscle cars battled to maintain relevance and dominance. These high-performance coupes with large, powerful V-8 engines and rear-wheel drive had been designed to satisfy our desire for power above all else. But the introduction of the Clean Air Act of 1970 forced automakers to drastically reduce emission pollutants. Clean air equipment became the new focus, robbing engines of much of their raw power and performance.

The better small car.
1971 Mercury Comet GT.

American auto makers responded to the stricter federal requirements, and to the increased competition from imports, by creating compact, more fuel-efficient car models. However, poor design, faulty engineering and substandard manufacturing led to a stream of road accidents and other disasters, damaging the customer experience.

Six car-producing countries dominated the industry in 1971: Japan, Germany, England, France and Italy, with America in the top spot.

Japan's recent rise into this elite group had been particularly aggressive, and their cars stood poised to dominate the world markets.

Japanese cars were affordable, reliable, compact, efficient and popular, quickly making Mazda, Nissan, Toyota, Mitsubishi, Datsun and Honda the export market leaders. Japanese car exports increased nearly 200-fold from start to end of the '60s.

Introducing the Toyota Celica ST.
[Some economy car.]

Volkswagen's Beetle remained popular, as it had been throughout the 1960s. Buyers tended to view German and Japanese cars as more reliable, safer and more fuel-efficient.

Today, you have good reason to see your SAAB dealer's full line of well-built Swedes.

Imports of foreign cars now made up 14.6% of American new car sales.

Advertisement

'71 Chevelle. How do you change America's most popular mid-size car?

1971. You've changed. We've changed.

Very carefully. You'd be surprised at all the advice we get. Some of it comes from our engineers, our stylists, our safety experts, our dealers, our stockholders. Even some from people we pay solely for advice: researchers.

But a lot of it comes from you. There's a lot you've always liked about Cheville. However one of the things you wanted for '71 was some new colors. We offer you 13 of them, all brand-new shades.

We contoured a new grille, and front and rear bumpers. Again, carefully. Very carefully. Put in new Power-Beam headlights. Single uncluttered units. Simple but effective. Effective, too, in our drive for clean air is our new Evaporation Control System. It uses absorbent charcoal to help keep carburetor and gas-tank evaporation out of the atmosphere.

While inside we provide you a new steering wheel with a cushioned center, and new control knobs wrapped in soft vinyl.

The whole idea is to keep Chevelle as popular with you as its price is.

Advertisement

Clean Air for All

Driver wearing a smog mask in the early '70s, Los Angeles, USA.

Our love affair with gas-guzzling, pollutant-emitting cars caused our air quality to deteriorate to severely unhealthy levels throughout the '50s and '60s. By the early '70s, pollutants from exhaust and industries left major cities regularly blanketed in a hazardous thick brown haze.

By 1972, the Clean Air Act (passed 31st December 1970) had become a serious concern for car manufacturers. The Act required leaded petrol engines to be phased out, and new vehicles to be engineered for cleaner emissions and fuel efficiency.

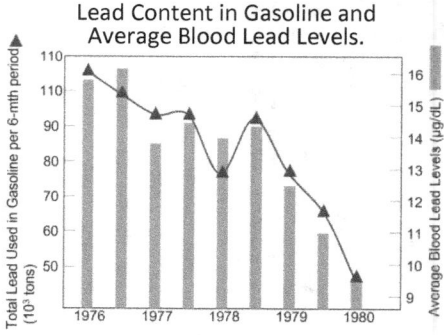

The Act required a 90% reduction of emissions from new automobiles within five years, targeting six major public health pollutants, including lead and carbon monoxide.

The US Environmental Protection Agency gave the states a short five years to meet these clean air quality goals, forcing the states to put pressure on industry and vehicle manufacturers.

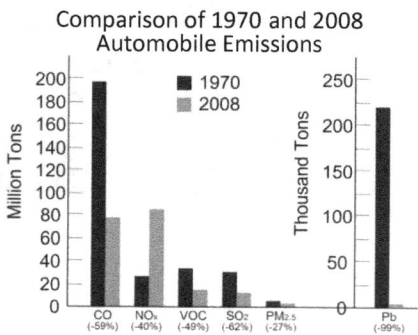

The UK implemented their first Clean Air Act in 1956. Their revised Act of 1970 specifically targeted carbon monoxide and hydrocarbons from automobile engines.

In Canada, Australia, and across Europe, similar legislations were developed throughout the '70s to tackle the undeniable problem of automobile-created photochemical smog which affected all major cities.

Different countries set their own standards, some more stringent than others. They also created their own methods for emissions testing of vehicles prior to sale, and of air quality testing for cities.

L.A. Grand Avenue in 1967 and now.

London's Great Fog of 1952 resulted in the deaths of 12,000 Londoners.

New York aerial view in 1973 and now.

Greenpeace Takes to the Seas

15th September 1971

The crew of the Phyllis Cormack (also called "Greenpeace") on-board the ship. Clockwise from top left: Hunter, Moore, Cummings, Metcalfe, Birmingham, Cormack, Darnell, Simmons, Bohlen, Thurston, and Fineberg. September 1971.

On 15th September 1971, a small group of concerned activists set sail from Vancouver to the Alaskan island of Amchitka to protest US nuclear testing taking place there. While waiting near the testing site, they stumbled upon a disused fishing village and whaling station. The discarded whale bones gave them the idea for their next campaign.

The organization Greenpeace was soon formed, with the aim of merging the anti-war movement with the environmental movement. By targeting human or political actions that harm the environment, Greenpeace activists were prepared to put themselves in harms way, protesting through peaceful resistance or direct confrontation.

Greenpeace's early anti-whaling campaigns received extensive TV coverage. Activists were shown sandwiched between giant whaling trawlers and bloody harpooned whales. Membership skyrocketed.

Today Greenpeace has offices in over 40 countries, tackling diverse issues from protecting the oceans, forests and endangered animals, to fighting climate change and toxic waste dumping.

Nuclear Bomb Testing

US underwater nuclear test at Bikini Atoll, 1946.

Remember when dropping nuclear bombs was commonplace? For more than 40 years, the Nuclear Arms Race gave the USA and USSR the pretext needed to test nuclear bombs on a massive scale. Nearly 1,700 bombs were dropped by the Superpowers, most of them during the decades of the '60s and '70s. A further 300 were tested by China, France, and the UK.

A partial Nuclear Test Ban Treaty in 1963 limited bomb testing in the atmosphere, in space, and under the ocean, making underground testing the standard for the next 3 decades.

These tests served to understand the effectiveness and capacity of each bomb type. They also acted as a deterrent to enemy nations.

In 1971 the US carried out 24 nuclear tests, mostly at the Nevada Proving Grounds, while USSR tested 23 nuclear bombs.

US troops and observers witness the detonation of *Small Boy* at the Nevada Proving Grounds, prior to the Test Ban, 1962.

Although most of the test sites were largely uninhabited by humans, some of them were densely populated. The effects of radioactive fallout plagued local populations for years afterwards.

Advertisement

"If I join the Women's Army Corps they'll cut off my hair."

Some girls believe the myth that the Women's Army Corps will try to make foot soldiers out of them. Cut their hair. And give them a baggy uniform.

Well, that's just plain nonsense.

Off duty or on, a girl can tint, tease, frost, iron her hair, or top it off with a new wig.

So there's never a hang-up with hair. There's even a place for your wig stand.

We know how special a girl's hair is to her total look. After all, we're girls, too. And we wouldn't dream of telling her how to wear it.

We do have one very practical rule that says hair should be kept above the collar while on duty. Just like any professional girl in uniform.

And there's one big regulation about the uniforms—that they make a girl look like one! It's her patriotic duty to stay looking trim and attractive.

A girl in the Women's Army Corps looks great because she feels great. About the world of travel, new friends, and job opportunities she's discovered.

Send the coupon, and we'll share it with you.

Or write: Army Opportunities, Department 400/450A, Hampton, Virginia 23369.

Please indicate education in your letter or coupon.

Your world is bigger in the Women's Army Corps.

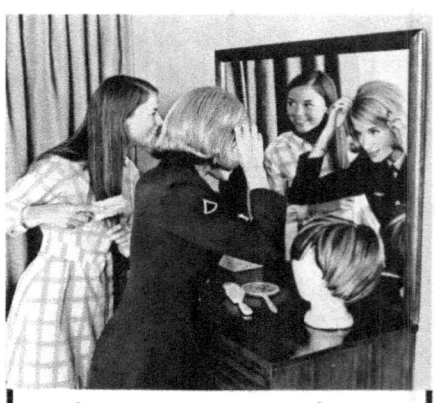

```
Army Opportunities                    Date_____
Dept. 400/450, Hampton, Va. 23369
Please send me more information on opportunities in the
Women's Army Corps. (Check one)
I am a ☐ high school student or ☐ graduate.
I am a ☐ college student or ☐ graduate.
Name_____ Date of Birth_____
Address_____
City_____ County_____
State_____ Zip Code_____ Phone_____
Date Graduated_____ Will Graduate On_____
                                              4C13-71
```

Anti-Vietnam War Sentiment 1955–1975

We had long ago grown tired and fed-up with the ongoing Vietnam War (known in Vietnam as the American War). By 1971, 156,800 US troops remained in Vietnam, with an additional 53,850 allied troops from South Korea, Thailand, Australia and New Zealand.[1]

Anti-war sentiment had been escalating during the previous few years, as more and more protestors took to the streets against what they believed to be an immoral war.

Numerous anti-war marches and civil disobedience campaigns were waged throughout the months of March and April, culminating with a 500,000 strong march on 24th April 1971 in Washington D.C. At the same time 150,000 marched in San Francisco.

Within weeks, the May Day protests began with the militant aim of bringing D.C. to a standstill. Protestors blocked roads, bridges and buildings. Police charged and fired tear gas, arresting 12,000 protesters over 3 days. It was the largest mass arrest in American history.

Actress Jane Fonda, the war's most high-profile critic, earned the nickname "Hanoi Jane" for her outspoken activism.

Forced to fight a war they didn't believe in, morale among the draftees was low. Drug usage became rampant. It is estimated up to 50% of US soldiers experimented with marijuana, opium and heroin, cheaply available on the streets of Saigon. US military hospitals would later report drug abuse victims far outnumbered actual war casualties.

[1] americanwarlibrary.com/vietnam/vwatl.htm.

Pentagon Papers White House Scandal — June 1971

On 13th June 1971, the New York Times ran a series of leaked articles exposing the truth about US political and military involvement in Vietnam, Cambodia and Laos from 1945 to 1967. The articles were excerpts from a 3,000-page secret Department of Defense report known as the Pentagon Papers.

Among other things, the report highlighted the extent to which successive governments had systematically lied to the American people and to Congress. It traced the covert actions of the military and the CIA in Indochina under Presidents Truman, Eisenhower, Kennedy, and Johnson. It exposed the misinformation spread to the American public to keep them engaged in a war they did not wholly believe in.

Newspaper headlines from June 1971.

The New York Times printed just three articles before the Nixon administration forced the paper to cease printing. The Washington Post began publishing articles on 18th June. They were met with a similar injunction to cease printing. Meanwhile several other papers received similar leaked articles and confirmed their intent to print.

On 30th June, the Supreme Court ruled that the media could print any articles they deemed newsworthy. Charges against Daniel Ellsberg, the researcher who had leaked the report, were eventually dropped.

Advertisement

When in Europe do as the Europeans do. Fly BEA.

EUROPE'S N°1 AIRLINE

Ask The French. Ask The Italians. Ask Any Mediterranean. BEA rates No.1 with them. We've a flying start with over 90 destinations. More flights to more places than any other European airline. That's experience! Yes, we go south, we go north, we go west. We'll really show you all around Europe. To all the big-time sophisticated cities. Berlin. Amsterdam. Copenhagen. Even Moscow. (Traveling BEA really widens your horizons.)

Or how about a game of hide and seek? Out of the way is right on our way. BEA wings you to places where pleasure is never crowded out. To Austria's Tyrol. To Oslo, home of the Vikings. Or go island hopping. To our own Western Isles.

Or the lemon-scented Greek islands. These are the spices of Europe. To miss them is to miss the authentic European flavor. And, of course, ask your fellow Americans. They'll tell you BEA talks your language. Not only is English spoken by our friendly cabin crews but in over 90 offices throughout Europe. (Wherever our passengers are stopped by a language gap—we bridge it.) Come on, jet ahead of everyone.

Our Tridents and BAC Super One Elevens powered by Rolls-Royce engines are so quiet, you'll think they're purring. Take a tip from the people who live or love Europe. BEA is the only way to go!

Ask Any Travel Agent. He knows BEA shows you Europe as you would show a friend around your home. No wonder so many Americans fly BEA... British European Airways.

Space Missions of 1971

Space missions did not stall after NASA's Apollo 11 historic man-on-the-moon mission. America's claim to have won the Space Race did not stop them, or the Soviets, from ongoing space exploration. In fact, the goals simply shifted. Having conquered the moon, what was next?

NASA continued taking astronauts to the moon, successfully landing two more spacecraft during 1971.

On 9th Feb, Apollo 14 became the third successful NASA moon mission. Astronauts Alan Shepard and Edgar Mitchell performed 9 hours of moon walks, bringing home 98 pounds of lunar material.

Crew of the Apollo 14: Stuart A. Roosa, Alan B. Shepard Jr. and Edgar D. Mitchell.

James Irwin salutes the American flag in front of the landing module and rover, 2nd August 1971.

Apollo 15 launched 26th July. Astronauts Jim Iwrin and David Scott spent 67 hours on the moon's surface. A Lunar Roving Vehicle, the first of its kind, was used to collect 173 pounds of moon rock.

Launch of Atlas-Centaur carrying Mariner 9.

In addition to the moon missions, NASA had also been developing robotic probes since 1963. The Mariner program focused on exploring Mars, Venus and Mercury.

Eight Mariner missions were carried out during the '60s to various degrees of success. Mariner 9, launched 30th May 1971, reached Mars after 6 months of traveling, becoming the first spacecraft to orbit another planet.

During its 349 days in orbit, Mariner 9 sent back over 7,000 images, mapping 85% of the surface of Mars.

The USSR abandoned plans to land on the moon after America's success in 1969. Their focus immediately shifted to developing a space station capable of supporting humans for extended periods in space. And to destinations further afield.

Diagram showing a Soyuz craft (rear) docking with the Salyut 1 (front).

The Soviet's Salyut 1 launched into low earth orbit on 19th April 1971, becoming the world's first space station. It received the 3-man crew of Soyuz 11 on 7th June. The cosmonauts remained on board for 22 days, orbiting the earth 362 times.

Within seconds of their return craft entering the Earth's atmosphere, the air-tight hatch seals failed, killing all 3 cosmonauts within.

The Salyut 1 was intentionally destroyed after 6 months in orbit, to be replaced by seven more space stations during the 15-year Salyut program. The program was vital for developing space station technology.

The Soviets set their goals even further when they launched two identical probes headed for Mars in March 1971. The Mars 2 and Mars 3 probes were orbiters with attached landers.

Soyez 11 Cosmonauts Georgy Dobrovolsky, Vladislav Volkov and Viktor Patsayev commemorated on a 1971 Soviet post stamp.

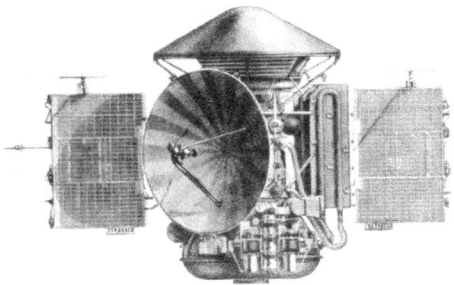

Diagram of Mars 2 (and identical Mars 3) orbiter with its lander on top.

The Mars 2 lander crash-landed on Mars, loosing contact with Earth. The Mars 3 lander successfully soft-landed on 2nd Dec 1971. It transmitted for just 20 secs. It is not sure if its rover was deployed.

Both orbiters successfully sent data and photos back to Earth from December 1971 until March 1972.

Advertisement

Springtime!
It happens every Salem.
Natural Menthol.
Not the artificial kind. That's what gives Salem a taste as fresh as Springtime. It's only natural.

Clairol
Frees the 'fro
A Kindness Instant Hairsetter styles it high, wide and easy to comb.
In just 15 minutes. Without hot combs or harsh chemicals.

This side was shaped with a comb.

This side was set with the Kindness Spray-and-Roll System.

Troubles in Northern Ireland 4th May 1971

"The Troubles" was a 30-year-long nationalist campaign, or low-level war, waged by Northern Irish Roman Catholic Republicans against the British (Protestant) Ulster Unionists. Although often mistaken for a war of religion, it was in fact a political war. The Republicans were fighting for the reunification of Northern Ireland with the Republic of Ireland. The Unionists were determined to keep Northern Ireland as part of the United Kingdom.

The Troubles flared up in the late '60s with local violence between the two factions. British Troops arrived to quell the situation, remaining for 37 years. Although their role was to be neutral peace-keepers, they were soon condemned for covertly supporting the Unionists.

British Troops arrest a suspected Republican, 6th Aug 1971.

A section of Peace Wall.

Peace Walls were hastily erected throughout the cities and suburbs of Northern Ireland, physically separating Republicans from Unionist neighborhoods.

A total of 21 miles (34 km) of Peace Walls were built by the British Government, which in recent years have become something of a tourist attraction.

A Northern Ireland commitment has been made to remove all the Peace Walls.

From 1971 to 1973 the political violence escalated. Republican paramilitaries commonly used guerilla tactics and bombing campaigns against British infrastructure, commercial and political targets, while Unionists attacked the wider Catholic community in "retaliation". A secret British Army unit, the Military Reaction Force, carried out undercover drive-by shootings against unarmed Catholic civilians.

9th August 1971– The British Government legalized internment (imprisonment without trial). Four days of violence followed resulting in the deaths of 20 civilians—all of them Catholic. Many reported physical and verbal abuse at the hands of the British troops. Many became radicalized as a result. British troops imprisoned nearly 350 people suspected of Republican paramilitary involvement under the internment laws.

Suspected Republicans rounded up for internment.

British troops during Bloody Sunday riots.

4th December 1971– Unionist paramilitaries bombed McGurk's Bar in Belfast, Northern Ireland. 15 Catholic civilians died when the building collapsed.

The bomb sparked a series of retaliatory attacks from both sides, culminating in the Bloody Sunday massacre of January 1972, when British Troops shot 26 civilians, killing 14, in full view of the public and press.

Throughout 1972, the worst year of the Troubles, nearly 500 people would lose their lives.

Bangladesh War of Independence 16th-25th July 1971

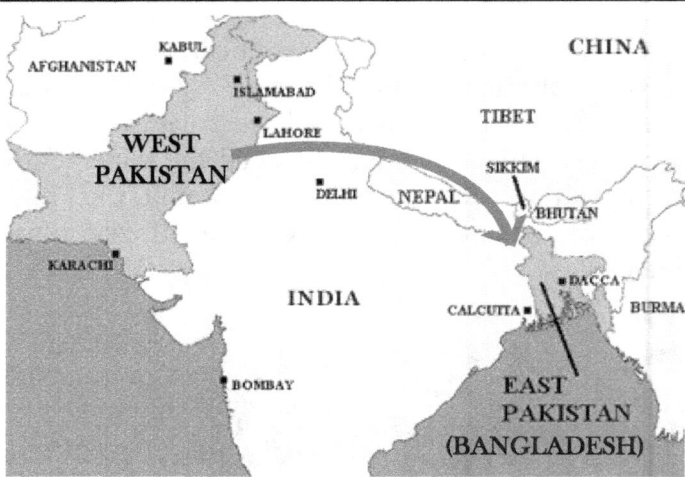

Bangladesh (formerly East Pakistan) is unique in the world, having been given a seat in the UN after unilaterally declaring independence from (West) Pakistan.

In March 1971, after 24 turbulent years in a forced union with West Pakistan, Bangladesh declared independence. Although separated by geography, politics, language and culture, the larger and more powerful western region was not prepared to release its renegade eastern state. Government forces were sent to enforce the union. Reports of mass atrocities, including genocide, changed international opinion in favor of the Bengali cause.

Pakistan Generals sign the Instrument of Surrender, 16th Dec 1971.

On 3rd December 1971, India entered the conflict, sending troops to assist the Bengalis. Within two weeks they had forced West Pakistan to accept defeat.

India formally recognized Bangladesh as a separate nation, leading other countries to do the same. In 1974 Bangladesh joined the UN, cementing its status as an independent country.

Advertisement

SPECIAL OFFER FROM KODAK.
SMILE SAVER KIT.

SPECIAL: You get a handsome, convenient travel case for your X-15.

SPECIAL: You get three self-powered Sylvania Blue Dot magicubes for twelve flash pictures.

SPECIAL: You get a Smile Saver pocket picture album.

Snap and save, now. Kodak makes this extra-special offer – for a limited time only – to introduce the camera that takes flash pictures without flash batteries. You get everything you need including Kodacolor-X film and the new Kodak Instamatic' X-15 camera. Just drop in the film. Pop on a magicube. And snap and save. A great gift idea, too.

COMPLETE GIFT OUTFIT. LESS THAN $25.

Kodak makes your pictures count.

Snap and save, now. Kodak makes this extra-special offer–for a limited time only–to introduce the camera that takes flash picture without flash batteries. You get everything you need including Kodacolor-X film and the new Kodak Instamatic X-15 camera. Just drop in the film. Pop on a magicube. And snap and save. A great gift idea, too.

Special: You get a handsome, convenient travel case for your X-15
Special: You get three self-powered Sylvania Blue Dot magicubes for twelve flash pictures.
Special: You get a Smile Saver pocket picture album.

Kodak makes your pictures count.

Death Sentence for Charles Manson   25th January 1971

Charles Manson in custody.

On 25th January, Charles Manson and three female members of his cult "family" were found guilty of first-degree murder. They would be sentenced to death by gas chamber on 19th April.

Charles Manson was the leader of "the family", a San Francisco based hippie cult of mostly female followers. He preached an apocalyptic war he called "Helter Skelter" would soon occur, where blacks would kill all the whites leaving only his family as the rulers of the earth.

In 1969 Manson ordered his followers to start Helter Skelter. Susan Atkins, Patricia Krenwinkel, and Charles "Tex" Watson, with Linda Kasabian as their driver, were sent to the home of Hollywood actress Sharon Tate, wife of director Roman Polanski. Tate, heavily pregnant at the time, and four of her guests were brutally murdered.

Sharon Tate in 1969.

1971 mug shots for Susan Atkins, Patricia Krenwinkel, Leslie Van Houten, and Tex Watson.

The following night Manson led the same four, plus Leslie Van Houten, to another home where they murdered Leno and Rosemary LaBianca. Two days later Kasabian fled the family. She would later testify as chief witness in their murder trials.

The Tate LaBianca murderers would eventually be caught and tried. Manson carved a swastika on his forehead, while Atkins, Krenwinkel, and Van Houten laughed throughout their trial. Watson was tried separately. They were all found guilty and received death sentences. In 1972, the death sentences were changed to life in prison.

Advertisement

The Dream Machine. $149.95

Now, Singer, the sewing people, guarantee you pleasant dreams at a price that's not a nightmare.

We admit it. There are other TV/digital clock-radio combinations. But they all do less. And they all cost more. • Our Big Difference. The others eliminate freedom of choice: If you want to wake up to radio you have to go to sleep to radio. Same with TV. Not The Dream Machine: the new Singer TV/FM-AM/Digital Clock Combination. It's the one-and-only one that *lets you set the media to suit your mood*. It lets you go to sleep watching TV and wake up to radio. Or vice-a-versa. Believe us: If anybody else did that they'd tell you about it. • Extra *"z-z-z-z-z's"*: Our Slumber Control lets you get those extra winks. • *Easy on the ears:* We've got two speakers. And a separate tone control, too. Plus an earphone jack for privacy. • That's not all. *Our 24-hour system:* Our digital clock's a 24-hour clock. That means you set it once for all time. Means the radio you set to wake you at 7:00 AM wont go off in the middle of dinner at 7:00 PM. • And "things that go bump in the night" won't be you. Our radio dial and your digital clock both have a *built-in nightlight*. • *Easy on the eyes:* Night and day this is the one. The only one with a *removable sun-screen*. Cuts glare. • *360° Swivel Base*–Another Exclusive–Lets you turn it to suit your eyes or your ears without picking it up. Or pushing it around. Nice!

There's More In Store For You At Singer

Walt Disney World Opens   1st October 1971

With the highly successful Disneyland theme park in California now 16 years old, Walt Disney Company's second theme park opened on 1st October 1971 in Orlando, Florida.

Thousands of balloons released to celebrate Walt Disney World's grand opening.

The Magic Kingdom with performers.

The original 1971 Magic Kingdom park with two hotels has now grown into a cluster of 4 themed parks plus 2 water parks, and over 25 resort hotels. The expansions continue to bring in new attractions while constantly upgrading existing favorites.

Although Walt Disney died in 1966 during the initial stages of planning, his brother and business partner, Roy O. Disney, worked tirelessly to ensure Walt's dream would come to fruition. Roy died just three months after the park's opening at 78 years old.

Jesus Christ Superstar on Broadway

12th October 1971

Composed by a very young Andrew Lloyd Webber, with lyrics by Tim Rice, the rock-opera theatrical sensation *Jesus Christ Superstar* was first released as a concept album a year before its stage debut on Broadway in October 1971. It won Webber a Drama Desk Award for the *Most Promising Composer*, which was to prove well earned. He would become one of musical theatre's most celebrated composers, with mega-hits such as *Phantom of the Opera, Cats, Evita*, and *School of Rock*.

Andrew Lloyd Webber receives Kennedy Center Honors in 2006.

Told through the eyes of Judas Iscariot, the musical's controversial interpretation of Jesus' last few days on earth, the compassion given to Judas, and the portrayal of the Jews as the villains, caused the musical to be condemned by many religious groups and banned in some countries.

Photos from the original Broadway cast of 1971.
Left: Roman soldiers carrying Jesus.
Right: Judas with Pharisees.

Scene from the last supper.

The production would open in London the following year with sell-out shows, becoming the longest running musical on the West End at that time.

Since then, *Jesus Christ Superstar* has been translated and performed on stage and in arenas around the world. It has also been showcased several times on TV and on film.

1971 in Cinema and Film

As cinema-goers, our interests and focus had shifted away from traditional classic Hollywood standards, which were often bounding with optimism and happy endings. We were seeking movies that offered more depth, more pain and a sense of reality.

By 1971, a new breed of directors like Francis Ford Coppola and Martin Scorsese demanded more artistic control. They bravely tackled darker, more gritty and more pessimistic themes of war, crime and depression. The era of big cinema houses owning their actors and controlling their directors had ended.

A new generation of brooding method-style actors rose to replace the retiring golden-era stars. Dustin Hoffman, Robert De Niro, Meryl Streep, Al Pacino, Jack Nicholson and Harvey Keitel are some of our enduring favorites.

Al Pacino in *Panic in Needle Park* (20th Century Fox, 1971).

Jack Nicholson and Candice Bergen in *Carnal Knowledge* (Embassy Pictures, 1971).

1971 film debuts

Kathy Bates	Taking Off
Stockard Channing	The Hospital
Daniel Day-Lewis	Sunday Bloody Sunday
Gérard Depardieu	Cry of the Cormoran
Cybill Shepherd	The Last Picture Show
Jacki Weaver	Stork

* From en.wikipedia.org/wiki/1971_in_film.

Top Grossing Films of the Year

 1 Fiddler on the Roof   United Artists $40,500,000
 2 Billy Jack   Warner Bros. $32,500,000
 3 The French Connection   20th Century Fox $26,300,000
 4 Summer of '42   Warner Bros. $20,500,000
 5 Diamonds Are Forever   United Artists $19,727,000
 6 Dirty Harry   Warner Bros. $18,000,000
 7 A Clockwork Orange   Warner Bros. $17,000,000
 8 Carnal Knowledge   Embassy Pictures $14,075,000
 9 The Last Picture Show   Columbia Pictures $13,110,000
10 Willard   Cinerama Releasing Corp. $9,300,000

* From en.wikipedia.org/wiki/1971_in_film by box office gross in the USA.

Stanley Kubrick's disturbing dystopian crime film *A Clockwork Orange* won the New York Film Critics Award, despite sexually explicit scenes causing it to be banned in numerous countries.

The French Connection won five out of eight Oscar nominations, including Best Picture, Best Director (for William Friedkin), and Best Actor (for Gene Hackman).

A Decade of Disasters

The Poseidon Adventure (20th Century Fox, 1972).

The Towering Inferno (20th Century Fox, 1974).

The decade of the '70s saw the disaster movie genre reign supreme at the box office. Large casts, multiple plot lines, life or death calamities and tales of survival kept us on the edge of our seats.

Earthquake (Universal, 1974).

Tidalwave (Toho, 1973).

Advertisement

AKAI AMERICA, LTD.

AKAI ELECTRIC CO., LTD.

AKAI's X-330 Stereo Tape Recorder is the ultimate for those who seek highest sound quality for long hours. This multipurpose tape recorder incorporates precision-processed professional mechanisms of ultra-durability. The Cross-Field Head incorporated in the X-330 is AKAI's unique recording head that gives you true sound reproduction. This exclusive and world-patented head has created a sensation in the tape recorder world by offering one of the widest recording ranges available today. And high fidelity recording can be attained even at the very slow speed of $1^7/_8$ ips.

Our X-330 is strictly for the professionals. With the use of $10^1/_2$ inch reels, the maximum continuous recording time is 24 hours monaural and 12 hours stereo. Continuous playback can be performed as long as you like with its automatic continuous reverse. This tape recorder also boasts sensing tape continuous reverse, manual reverse, 4 heads, 3 motors, 3 speeds, automatic stop/shut off, and magnetic brake. AKAI's X-330D Stereo Tape Deck is also available.

Other AKAI products incorporating its unique Cross-Field Head include the M-10 Stereo Tape Recorder and the X-220D Stereo Tape Deck. The M-10 features 3 heads, 3 motors, 3 speeds, automatic continuous reverse with sensing tape, manual reverse, automatic stop/shut off, and instant stop control. The X-220 features 3 heads, 3 motors, 3 speeds, automatic continuous reverse with sensing tape, manual reverse, automatic stop/shut off, and instant stop control and solid state pre-amplifier with two integrated circuits.

Musical Memories

1971 was a golden year for rock. The Beatles had just split up, we had turned our backs on '60s psychedelic rock and silly love songs, and some of the most influential music and albums of our lifetime were recorded. Musicians were writing, recording, and performing at a blistering pace.

A new generation of singer-songwriters were penning lyrics about serious social and personal issues. Carole King's *Tapestry* stayed at #1 on Billboard for 15 weeks. Joni Mitchell's *Blue* was listed #3 on *Rolling Stone* magazine's *500 Greatest Albums of All Time* (2020). Led Zeppelin's *IV,* featuring their signature song *Stairway to Heaven*, defined the mood and style of '70s Hard Rock.

Other influential records included *Who's Next* by The Who, *Master of Reality* by Black Sabbath, *L.A. Women* by The Doors, *Sticky Fingers* by The Rollings Stones, *Every Picture Tells A Story* by Rod Stewart, *Carly Simon* by Carly Simon, and *American Pie* by Don McLean.

Marvin Gaye's groundbreaking album *What's Going On* explored hatred, suffering, injustice, poverty and drug abuse from the viewpoint of a returning Vietnam Vet. It was a marked departure from the usual Motown sound.

John Lennon's single *Imagine* was released on 8th October, from the album of the same name. It would become the biggest selling single of his solo career and an enduring anthem of peace, love and social change.

The first Glastonbury Festival (Somerset, UK) was held from 20th-24th June to coincide with the summer solstice. Money was put up and the land provided to ensure the event remained free to festival goers.

The temperamental British weather remained largely fine as a crowd of 7,000 gathered. Although not considered huge, the festival was a success, with David Bowie headlining the twenty-act line-up.

As the festival was not a money-making affair, it would not become a yearly event until the 1980s.

The signature steel-structure pyramid stage, first erected in 1971, continues to appear today in modified and updated forms.

At the same time, the Celebration of Life festival in McCrae (Louisiana, USA) suffered untold disasters. Poor organization left the site unsecured till 4 days before the event. None of the promised big-name acts showed up, reducing the eight-day festival to just four days.

An abundance of drugs and mosquitoes, and lack of toilets, food and water, made conditions unbearable. The extreme heat forced bands to perform only at night. Gale force winds blew down part of the stage. And at day's end, three were dead from drugs and drowning.

In other news:

12th May– Mick Jagger married Bianca Pérez-Mora Macías in Paris.

3rd Jul– Jim Morrison, aged 27, was found dead in his bathtub in Paris. The official cause of death was heart failure, although numerous eyewitnesses believe an accidental heroin overdose was to blame.

1971 Billboard Top 30 Songs

	Artist	Song Title
1	Three Dog Night	Joy to the World
2	Rod Stewart	Maggie May / Reason to Believe
3	Carole King	It's Too Late / I Feel the Earth Move
4	The Osmonds	One Bad Apple
5	Bee Gees	How Can You Mend a Broken Heart
6	Paul Revere & the Raiders	Indian Reservation
7	Donny Osmond	Go Away Little Girl
8	John Denver	Take Me Home, Country Roads
9	The Temptations	Just My Imagination (Running Away with Me)
10	Tony Orlando and Dawn	Knock Three Times

Rod Stuart, 1971.

The Osmonds, 1971.

John Denver, 1973.

The Bee Gees, 1973.

	Artist	Song Title
11	Janis Joplin	Me and Bobby McGee
12	Al Green	Tired of Being Alone
13	Honey Cone	Want Ads
14	The Undisputed Truth	Smiling Faces Sometimes
15	Cornelius Brothers & Sister Rose	Treat Her Like a Lady
16	James Taylor	You've Got a Friend
17	Jean Knight	Mr. Big Stuff
18	The Rolling Stones	Brown Sugar
19	Lee Michaels	Do You Know What I Mean
20	Joan Baez	The Night They Drove Old Dixie Down

Tom Jones, 1969.   The Carpenters, 1972.

	Artist	Song Title
21	Marvin Gaye	What's Going On
22	Paul & Linda McCartney	Uncle Albert/Admiral Halsey
23	Bill Withers	Ain't No Sunshine
24	Five Man Electrical Band	Signs
25	Tom Jones	She's a Lady
26	Murray Head & The Trinidad Singers	Superstar
27	The Free Movement	I've Found Someone of My Own
28	Jerry Reed	Amos Moses
29	The Grass Roots	Temptation Eyes
30	The Carpenters	Superstar

* From the *Billboard* top 30 singles of 1971.

Advertisement

The either-or stereo from JVC

Model 4344 is the latest pacesetter from JVC. With more features, more versatility than any other compact in its field. You can enjoy either its superb FM stereo/AM receiver. Or your favorite albums on its 4-speed changer. Or 4-track cassettes on its built-in player. Or you can record your own stereo cassettes direct from the radio, or use its microphones (included) to record from any outside source. And you get all these great components in a beautiful wooden cabinet that can sit on a book-shelf.

But don't let its size fool you — JVC's 4344 is a real heavyweight. With 45 watts music power, 2-way speaker switching and matching air suspension speakers, illuminated function indicators, handsome blackout dial, separate bass and treble controls, FM-AFC switch. Even two VU meters to simplify recording, and more.

See the Model 4344 at your nearest JVC dealer today. Or write us direct for his address and color brochure.

JVC Catching On Fast

JVC America, Inc., 50-35, 56th Road, Maspeth, New York, N.Y. 11378

Model 4344 is the latest pacesetter from JVC. With more features, more versatility than any other compact in its field. You can enjoy either its superb FM stereo/AM receiver. Or your favorite albums on its 4-speed changer. Or 4-track cassettes on its built-in player. Or you can record your own stereo cassettes direct from the radio, or use its microphones (included) to record from any outside source. And you get all these great components in a beautiful wooden cabinet that can sit on a book-shelf.

But don't let its size fool you–JVC's 4344 is a real heavyweight. With 45 watts music power, 2-way speaker switching and matching air suspension speakers, illuminated function indicators, handsome blackout dial, separate bass and treble controls, FM-AFC switch. Even two VU meters to simplify recording, and more.

See the Model 4344 at your nearest JVC dealer today. Or write us direct for his address and color brochure.

JVC Catching On Fast

Advertisement

How to kill yourself.

Eat! Drink! And Be Merry?
And whatever you do, by all means, overdo it.

Eat! It gives you something to do when you're bored or tense. (Sure, your doctor told you how many calories you should take in in a day. But it's been a long day.)

Drink! You don't really need it to unwind. It's just to be sociable.

A second helping of dessert? Lemon meringue pie is mostly egg white. And how about a pizza while you are watching TV after dinner? Of course, it always tastes better with beer.

What was it your doctor said? "People are the only animals who eat themselves to death." But you know it's your glands, not your appetite, that makes *you* plump.

Why Are America's Doctors Telling You This?
Well, for a long time we've been telling you how to stay alive and healthy. (Last year, 70% of the annual budget of the American Medical Association went to health and scientific education.) But many of you go do the opposite.

Now we figure we'll tell you how to kill yourselves. In the fervent hope that once again you'll do the exact opposite. If you do, there's every chance we'll be seeing less of you. Once a year for a checkup. And that's it.

Doing your bit to take care of yourself simply means your doctor can give everyone the best care possible. When *only* his care will do.

For a free booklet on eating and good health, write: American Medical Association, Box H, 535 North Dearborn Street, Chicago, Illinois 60610.

America's Doctors of Medicine

Eat! Drink! And Be Merry? And whatever you do, by all means, overdo it.

Eat! It gives you something to do when you're bored or tense. (Sure, your doctor told you how many calories you should take in in a day. But it's been a long day.)

Drink! You don't really need it to unwind. It's just to be sociable.

A second helping of dessert? Lemon meringue pie is mostly egg white. And how about a pizza while you are watching TV after dinner? Of course, it always tastes better with beer. What was it your doctor said? "People are the only animals who eat themselves to death." But you know it's your glands, not your appetite, that makes *you* plump.

Why Are America's Doctors Telling You This?

Well, for a long time we've been telling you how to stay alive and healthy. (Last year, 70% of the annual budget of the American medical Association went to health and scientific education.) But many of you go do the opposite. Now we figure we'll tell you how to kill yourselves. In the fervent hope that once again you'll do the exact opposite. If you do, there's every chance we'll be seeing less of you. Once a year for a checkup. And that's it. Doing your bit to take care of yourself simply means your doctor can give everyone the best care possible. When *only* his care will do.

America's Doctors of Medicine

Fashion Trends of the 1970s

By the early '70s, the fashion industry had lost its way, with designers and consumers alike seeking new directions and answers to the changing times. This was a decade without guidance and without rules. Trends caught on and shifted quickly. Fashions were varied and experimental. Pants got wider, skirts got shorter, and boots got taller. And within a season the trends reversed. Anything was possible, everything was acceptable.

Walking down any street you would have found skirts worn mini, midi, or full length. Pants could be slim-fit, wide, or bell bottomed, hip-hugging or waist-clinching. Tops might be tie-dye swirl-patterned or bold solids. Shirts came long and loose, or tight and tailored.

Daywear pants-suit and skirt-suit.

Dresses came in all shapes and lengths too. They could be short Mod shifts, or calico lace prairie-style. They could be tailored with shirt-style collars and buttoned-down fronts. They could be long and loose caftans, flowing maxi-dresses, or waisted tailored-cut with belts and A-line skirts taken straight from the '50s.

Patchwork maxi-dresses by Yves Saint Laurent.

The hippie and psychedelic fashions of the late '60s were adopted and modified by mainstream non-hippies into more elegant structured forms. Caftans, prairie dresses, patchwork fabrics, shawls, tassels and beads hit the runways, and the streets, in the early '70s.

Elizabeth Taylor during her bohemian period, 1969.

Maudie James models Thea Porter patchwork dress, 1970.

Weipert and Burda fashion show, 1972.

In contrast to the hippie trends, Mod dresses of the early '60s made a comeback. Space-age synthetics and plastics, widely used in the '60s, were replaced with comfortable cottons and stretch knits. In winter, tunic dresses could be worn over turtlenecks, with woolen stockings or thigh-high boots.

Mod mini dresses worn with white boots or shoes, early 1970s.

The '70s were the first full decade where pants for women gained mainstream acceptance, and we couldn't get enough of them. Pants could be worn for any occasion—pants-suits for the office, silky patterns for evenings, or blocks and geometrics dressed down for daywear. And let's not forget blue jeans, the staple of casual wear for both men and women.

Day wear pants from the Sears Spring/ Summer catalog, 1970.

In the early '70s men and women wore their pants gently flared at the base. As the decade progressed, the flares got wider and wider, exploding into bell-bottoms by the mid-'70s.

Embroidered denim.   Flared knit polyester pants.   Flared silky jumpsuits.

Advertisement

"There's a new man in my life."

There's a Car Man for every woman at **CITGO**

There's a Car Man for every woman at CITGO.

People think a bachelor girl like me has lots of men in her life. And I do. There's the milkman. The mailman. The laundry man. And now, there's a new man in my life... the Car Man at CITGO.

The Car man does more than just fill the tank with gasoline. He explains things to me. He told me that you rotate the tires for the same reason you flip a mattress. So they don't wear out in one place. The Car Man looks for trouble, too. The kind of trouble a woman doesn't even know can happen. Like when you don't change the oil.

The Car Man takes care of my whole car. And that makes me feel a lot better about driving. I just don't know what a girl like me would do without him. I think the Car Man makes CITGO an even nicer place to visit.

There's a Car Man for every woman at CITGO.

Shiny polyester Nik Nik shirts. Stretch polyester tops and flared pants. Terry toweling jumpsuits.

Caught between the hippie and mod fashion extremes of the early '70s, the rest of us settled for easy-care. Whether it was casual, formal or business attire, being easy to wash and drip-dry dictated what we wore. Non-iron wool jersey knits and non-iron polyester were the material of choice for men and women throughout the '70s.

The '70s are often considered to be the decade that fashion forgot (or the decade of fashion that we would rather forget). And it's not hard to see why. Anything and everything became acceptable, no matter how outlandish or mismatched.

Here are some of our more questionable fashion decisions from the decade.

Shiny stretch polyester jumpsuits. Denim on denim. Stretch knit pantsuits. Safari suits.

John Travolta in *Saturday Night Fever* (Paramount Pictures, 1977).

Dancer at Studio 54, New York.

And then there was disco.
It shone so brightly. It glittered so briefly.
And in a flash, it was gone.

Sporting silver lamé jumpsuits.

Dancers at Studio 54, New York.

Model wears sequined jumpsuit.

Advertisement

It takes beautiful close-up color portraits because that's all it takes.

Big faces—the kind of pictures you want most. The Polaroid Big Shot Land camera is only for close-up color portraits. That's why the camera looks so unusual—its length takes the place of expensive cameras with complicated lenses or special attachments. Pictures are almost all face, the kind you get in portrait studios.

Portraits that you can't mess up. Forget words like "focus" and "exposure." This is the simplest of all systems. You focus with your feet. Just walk toward your subject until the two faces in the window are one—and press the button.

Do not worry about lighting. It is the same, indoors and out. A flashcube behind a big diffusion panel gives you soft portrait lighting every shot. There are no settings. Not even batteries.

The timer signals when your picture is developed and ready to see—and that's it. So easy the kids can take <u>your</u> portrait.

Polaroid's $19.95*Big Shot.
If you can find one, Merry Christmas.

It takes beautiful close-up color portraits because that's all it takes.

Big faces–the kind of pictures you want most. The Polaroid Big Shot Land camera is only for close-up color portraits. That's why the camera looks so unusual–its length takes the place of expensive cameras with complicated lenses or special attachments. Pictures are almost all face, the kind you get in portrait studios.

Portraits that you can't mess up. Forget words like "focus" and "exposure." This is the simplest of all systems. You focus with your feet. Just walk toward your subject until the two faces in the window are one–and press the button.

Do not worry about lighting. It is the same, indoors and out. A flashcube behind a big diffusion panel gives you soft portrait lighting every shot. There are no settings. Not even batteries.

The timer signals when your picture is developed and ready to see–and that's it. SO easy the kids can take <u>your</u> portrait.

Polaroid's $19.95 Big Shot. If you can find one. Merry Christmas.

Also in Sports

2nd Jan– 66 football supporters were crushed to death in a stairwell at Ibrox Stadium (Glasgow, Scotland) as they tried to leave following a Rangers v Celtic match. A further 200 were injured.

5th Jan– The first one-day cricket international was played at Melbourne's MCG. Australia beat England by five wickets. The match was invented as a one-off event, after 3 days of rain forced the cancellation of a Test match.

8th Mar– Known as the "Fight of the Century", the highly anticipated battle between the two undefeated champions, Joe Frazier and Muhammad Ali, at Madison Square Garden, NYC, saw Frazier end Ali's 31-fight winning streak, (Ali had not fought since 1966). Frazer won in 15 rounds to retain the heavyweight boxing title.

3rd Jun– Imran Khan made his test cricket debut for Pakistan against England at Edgbaston, UK. (5, 0-36, 0-19).

Evonne Goolagong in 1971.

June-July– Australia ruled the summer in tennis with all-Australian Women's finals at the French Open (Evonne Goolagong beat Helen Gourlay, Women's Singles), and at Wimbledon (Evonne Goolagong beat Margaret Court, Women's Singles). Australia also won the Wimbledon Men's Singles (John Newcombe beat American Stan Smith).

American Tennis champion Billie Jean King became the first female athlete to earn over $100,000 in prize money in a single year. Despite her large paychecks, King fought tirelessly to secure equal prize money for men and women.

Advertisement

There are only six $25 electric watches made in the free world.
Timex makes them all.

You've probably been waiting to buy an electric watch for years. But the price stopped you. Now it won't. Because now you can have an Electric Timex at a beautiful price. Just $25. (And you can have just about any of the same styles with an automatic calendar for just $30.)

And you'll have all the benefits the name implies: Electric accuracy. The convenience of a watch that never needs winding. (A tiny replaceable energy cell powers the Electric Timex with steady electric accuracy for a whole year.) A rugged watch that's water resistant and dust resistant. And a choice of styles. You've been waiting for an affordable price? Now you have it.

The Electric Timex. It never needs winding.

Invention of the Electronic Mail

Of all the possibilities that the internet offers us, email remains the most widely used and arguably the most important application available. Just about everybody has one or more email addresses, and most individuals and business rely on email to maintain normal daily function.

Long before we had personal computers on every desk, email had already been invented. In 1971, Ray Tomlinson, working for Bolt Beranek and Newman, developed a way to send messages between users of different computers through a network known as ARPANET, (the precursor to the modern internet).

The first electronic mail was sent between these two adjacent PDP-10 computers at BBN Technologies (connected only through the ARPANET).

Ray Tomlinson in 2004.

Tomlinson selected the "at" symbol to separate the user's name from the computer's name.

With the invention of the World Wide Web, email became available and affordable to all. Usage exploded as hundreds of millions discovered the simplicity and benefits of communicating electronically.

Other News from 1971

2nd Jan– Cigarette advertising was banned from TV in the USA.

8th Feb– The NASDAQ stock exchange commenced trading as the world's first fully-automated electronic stock market.

9th Feb– A 6.6 magnitude earthquake in the San Fernando Valley killed 64 people, leaving $500 million in property damage.

San Fernando highway overpass collapse, 1971.

5th Apr– Mount Etna (Sicily, Italy), Europe's largest volcano, erupted at 7.30pm. Molten lava continued to spew from numerous fissures until mid-June, flowing up to 7.5 km away.

1st Jul– Debt raised to build San Francisco's Golden Gate Bridge was finally paid off. The funds were raised through construction bonds and paid for entirely by toll charges collected on the bridge.

1st Jul– The US lowered the voting age to 18-years-old.

1st Jul– Britain and Argentina signed an accord breaking the deadlock on communications, education, and medical supplies to the Falkland Islands. The UK continued its claim of sovereignty.

8th Sep– The John F. Kennedy Center for Performing Arts opened in Washington, D.C. with a gala performance and Requiem mass in honor of the late President Kennedy.

29th Sep– A cyclone and tidal wave off the Bay of Bengal killed as many as 10,000 on the eastern coast of India. The 6-foot tidal surge reached 30 miles inland, destroying electrical and telecommunication lines, roads, crops, and tens of thousands of houses.

12th Oct– The US House of Representatives approved the Equal Rights Amendment (1971) providing legal equality for women and banning discrimination based on sex. It was passed by Senate in March 1972.

21st Oct– The Nobel prize for literature was awarded to Chilean poet Pablo Neruda, two years before his sudden death. His official cause of death was listed as heart attack however it is widely believed he was murdered by the Pinochet regime.

31st Oct– Swiss women voted for the first time after gaining suffrage in February 1971.

21st Dec– The United Arab Emirates (UAE) was formed as a union of seven small kingdoms, gaining independence from the United Kingdom after nearly 80 years of British rule. The UAE is now famed for its natural reserves of oil and gas, and extremely wealthy and modern cities.

Remember when the Peace Corps happened?

There was an electricity, a shared smile. Most of us said, "What a great idea!" And thousands of Americans said, "I want in."

Just like that. The Peace Corps was in business, exporting a product that the cynics had made jokes about for two hundred years: The American Innocence, the notion that people can change things.

The supply of volunteers was unlimited. Before the Sixties ended more than 40,000 Americans — most of them young and white and college educated — had joined the Peace Corps.

Whatever happened to the Peace Corps?

What happened was that America, the world's leading exporter of innocence, ran out of the product at home. Let's not go through the list again. Growing up anytime, anywhere is hard work. Growing up in America has become almost unbearable.

The Peace Corps had some growing up to do, too.

It had to stop telling young people that love alone conquers all, because it doesn't.

It had to stop saying that volunteers could be "agents of change" — political change — because it wasn't true.

It had to stop pretending it wasn't a United States government agency, because it is.

It had to learn that — believe it or not — people in faraway lands know more about what they need than we do. (And when they ask for help, they're very specific: an electrician, two city planners, five math teachers, an experienced farmer.)

Today the Peace Corps is in 60 countries. That's 59 more than it started in. It's changed a lot, but so has the world and so has America, and so — after all — have you.

The Peace Corps is still a remarkable idea for people who need to help, nose to nose. But it's not like it used to be.

It's better.

Print advertisement for 10th year anniversary of the Peace Corps.

In 1961, during his first year in office, President Kennedy established the Peace Corps, a state funded organization which trained young American volunteers for deployment in foreign nations on two or three-year terms, with the goal of assisting developing nations in community development.

Asked "what you can do for your country," thousands volunteered. By 1971, 8500 volunteers were working on more than 500 projects in 60 third-world countries.

Advertisement

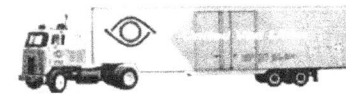

There are some things a woman can't ask a man

And who should know better than another woman? That's why United Van Lines' Bette Malone stays so busy answering questions and giving advice to the feminine members of the families we move. □ It may be a tip on selling your house. A list of school and medical records the kids will need. The best way to transport the family pooch. Or how to pack an unwieldy item so it'll arrive in one piece. □ For the woman who is wondering about her new home town, Bette Malone provides the intimate details–up-to-date facts about educational facilities, churches, shopping centers, taxes, climate and the other things you should know. □ This personalized service is free for the asking through your nearby United agent. Look him up in the Yellow Pages. Or drop a line to Bette Malone. She's the best friend a gal ever had on moving day.

We do more than get you there.

Famous People Born in 1971

17th Jan– Kid Rock (Robert James Ritchie), American rapper, songwriter, musician & actor.

20th Jan– Gary Barlow, English singer (Take That).

22nd Feb– Lea Salonga, Filipina singer & actress.

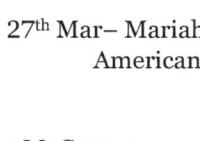

27th Mar– Mariah Carey, American singer.

31st Mar– Ewan McGregor, Scottish actor.

7th Apr– Guillaume Depardieu, French actor.

12th Apr– Shannen Doherty, American actress.

14th May– Sofia Coppola, American film director.

27th May– Paul Bettany, English actor.

28th May– Marco Rubio, American politician.

30th May– Idina Menzel, American actress & singer.

5th Jun– Mark Wahlberg, actor & rapper.

22nd Jun– Kurt Warner, American Pro Football Hall of Fame quarterback.

26th Jun– Max Biaggi, Italian Grand Prix motorcycle racer.

27th Jun– Jo Frost, British TV personality (Supernanny).

28th Jun– Elon Musk, American entrepreneur & inventor.

3rd Jul– Julian Assange, Australian founder of Wikileaks.

20th Jul– Sandra Oh, Korean Canadian actress.

12th Aug– Pete Sampras, American tennis player (14 Grand Slam titles).

20th Aug– David Walliams, English actor, comedian & children's author.

31st Aug– Chris Tucker, American stand-up comedian & actor.

8th Sep– David Arquette, American actor, director & producer.

8th Sep– Martin Freeman, English actor.

8th Sep– Lachlan Murdoch, Australian, British, American businessman (New Corp).

13th Sep– Goran Ivanišević, Croatian tennis player.

13th Sep– Stella Nina McCartney, English fashion designer & daughter of Paul McCartney

16th Sep– Amy Poehler, American comedian & actress.

18th Sep– Lance Armstrong, American road cyclist (7 Tour de France titles before banned).

18th Sep– Jada Pinkett Smith, American actress.

13th Oct– Sacha Baron Cohen, British comedian & actor.

20th Oct– Snoop Dogg [Calvin Broadus], American rapper.

29th Oct– Winona Ryder, American actress.

21st Nov– Michael Strahan, American Pro Football Hall of Fame & TV host.

Advertisement

The Come As You Are Party Tyme.

Get your friends off the ski slope, out of the barber chair, out of the deep blue sea, and over to your place for a last minute crazy fun party.

To go with the dazzling array of outfits, a dazzling array of Party Tyme Cocktails.

Banana Daiquiris, rich with a sweet tropical banana flavor. Fruity Mai Tais, Whiskey Sours, Margaritas. 13 different Party Tyme Cocktail Mixes in all.

And they're all so easy to fix, they practically come as they are.

Anytime is Party Tyme.

The Come As You Are Party Tyme.

Get your friends off the ski slope, out of the barber chair, out of the deep blue sea, and over to your place for a last minute crazy fun party.

To go with the dazzling array of outfits, a dazzling array of Party Tyme Cocktails.

Banana Daiquiris, rich with a sweet tropical banana flavor. Fruity Mai Tais, Whiskey Sours, Margaritas. 13 different Party Tyme Cocktail Mixes in all.

And they're all so easy to fix, they practically come as they are.

Party Tyme Cocktail Mixes. Anytime is Party Tyme.

1971 in Numbers

Census Statistics [1]:

- Population of the world   3.78 billion
- Population in the United States   211.38 million
- Population in the United Kingdom   55.75 million
- Population in Canada   21.72 million
- Population in Australia   13.03 million
- Average age for marriage of women   20.9 years old
- Average age for marriage of men   23.1 years old
- Average family income USA $9,030 per year
- Minimum wage USA $1.60 per hour

Costs of Goods [2]:

- Average new house — $26,216
- Average new car — $3,600
- Chevrolet Pickup — $2,229
- A gallon of gasoline — $0.36
- A loaf of bread — $0.25
- A gallon of milk — $1.32
- Frozen french fries — $0.69 per 5 pounds
- Sliced bacon — $0.69 per pound
- Fresh turkey — $0.69 per pound
- Potatoes — $0.12 per pound
- Fresh eggs — $0.53 per dozen
- Peanut butter — $0.59
- A cinema ticket — $1.65
- US Postage stamp — $0.08

---

[1] Figures taken from worldometers.info/world-population, US National Center for Health Statistics, *Divorce and Divorce Rates* US (cdc.gov/nchs/data/series/sr_21/sr21_029.pdf) and United States Census Bureau, *Historical Marital Status Tables* (census.gov/data/tables/time-series/demo/families/marital.html).
[2] Figures from thepeoplehistory.com, mclib.info/reference/local-history & dqydj.com/historical-home-prices/.

Hellmann's helps you bake from scratch without eggs or shortening
Mayonnaise Cake

Moist, luscious chocolate cake with no beating, no creaming. That's because creamy, rich Hellmann's replaces both eggs and shortening. Blends smoothly with a stir. That's real mayonnaise. Whole-egg Hellmann's.

Chocolate Mayonnaise Cake

- 3 cups unsifted flour
- 1 ½ cups sugar
- ⅓ cup cocoa
- 2 ¼ teaspoons baking powder
- 1 ½ teaspoons baking soda
- 1 ½ cups Hellmann's Real Mayonnaise
- 1 ½ cups water
- 1 ½ teaspoons vanilla

Grease 2 (9 x 1 ½-inch) layer pans; line bottoms with waxed paper. Sift together dry ingredients into large bowl. Stir in Real Mayonnaise. Gradually stir in water and vanilla until smooth and blended. Pour into prepared pans. Bake in 350°F. (moderate) oven about 30 minutes or until cake springs back when touched. Cool. Remove from pans. Makes 2 layers.

BRING OUT THE HELLMANN'S AND BRING OUT THE BEST

Bring out the Hellmann's and bring out the best

Advertisement

Daddy, what did you do in the war against pollution?

Of course you can always try to change the subject.

But one answer you can't give is that you weren't in it. Because in this war, there are no 4F's and no conscientious objectors. No deferments for married men or teen-agers. And no exemptions for women.

So like it or not, we're all in this one. But as the war heats up, millions of us stay coolly uninvolved. We have lots of alibis:

What can one person do?

It's up to "them" to do something about pollution – not me.

Besides, average people don't pollute. It's the corporations, institutions and municipalities.

The fact is that companies and governments are made up of people. It's people who make decisions and do things that foul up our water, land and air. And that goes for businessmen, government officials, housewives or homeowners.

What can one person do for the cause? Lots of things – maybe more than you think. Like cleaning your spark plugs every 1000 miles, using detergents in the recommended amounts, by upgrading incinerators to reduce smoke emissions, by proposing and supporting better waste treatment plants in your town. Yes, and throwing litter in a basket instead of in the street.

Above all, let's stop shifting the blame. People start pollution. People can stop it. When enough Americans realize this we'll have a fighting chance in the war against pollution.

People start pollution. People can stop it.

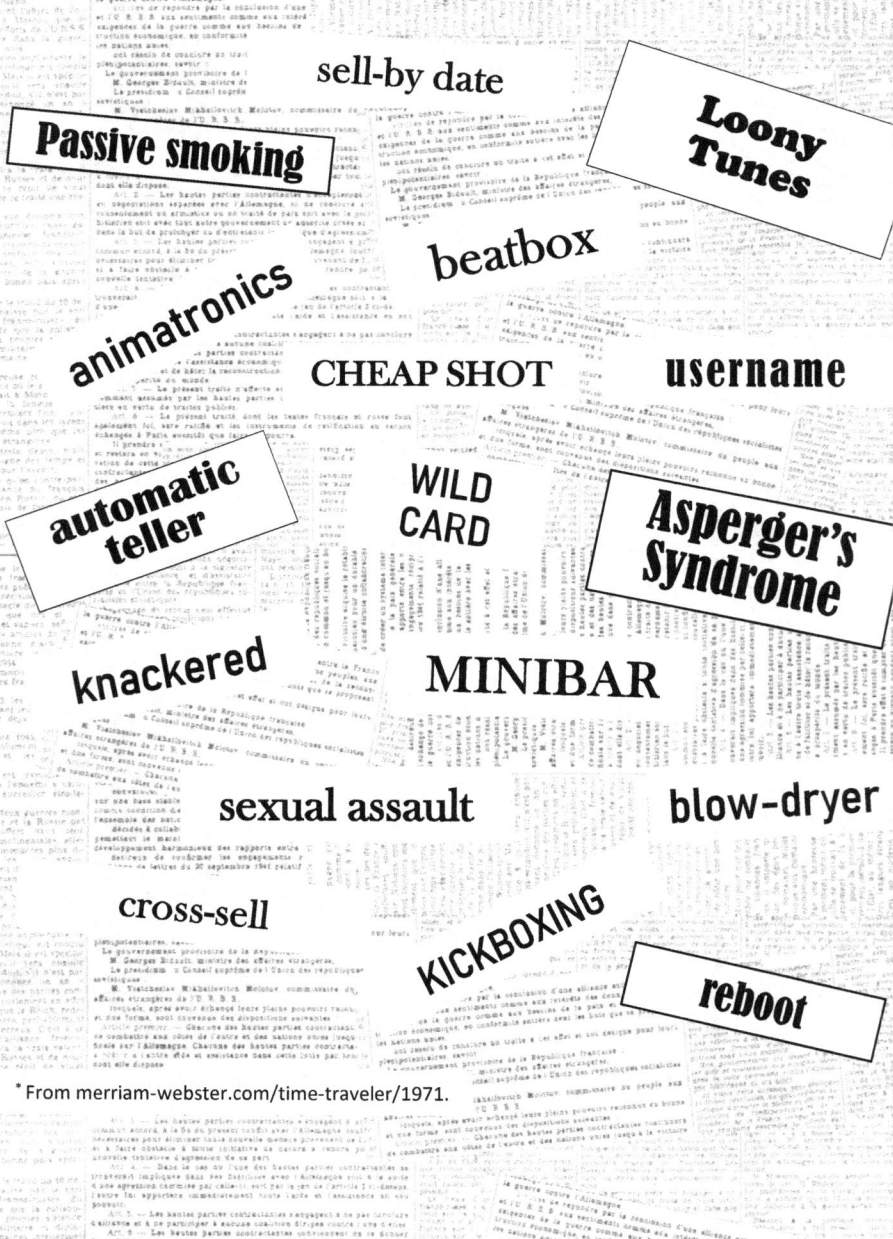

A heartfelt plea from the author:

I sincerely hope you enjoyed reading this book and that it brought back many fond memories from the past.

Success as an author has become increasingly difficult with the proliferation of **AI generated** copycat books by unscrupulous sellers. They are clever enough to escape copyright action and use dark web tactics to secure paid-for **fake reviews**, something I would never do.

Hence I would like to ask you—I plead with you—the reader, to leave a star rating or review on Amazon. This helps make my book discoverable for new readers, and helps me to compete fairly against the devious copycats.

If this book was a gift to you, you can leave stars or a review on your own Amazon account, or you can ask the gift-giver or a family member to do this on your behalf.

I have enjoyed researching and writing this book for you and would greatly appreciate your feedback.

Best regards,
Bernard Bradforsand-Tyler.

Please leave a
book review/rating at:

https://bit.ly/1971-reviews

Or scan the QR code:

Flashback books make the perfect gift- see the full range at

https://bit.ly/FlashbackSeries

Image Attributions

Photographs and images used in this book are reproduced courtesy of the following:

Page 6 – From *Life* Magazine 3rd Sept 1971.
Source: books.google.com/books?id=SkAEAAAAMBAJ&printsec (PD image).*
Page 8&9 – PD images from the U.S. News & World Report collection at the Library of Congress Prints and Photo division.
Page 10 – From *Life* Magazine 3rd Sept 1971.
Source: books.google.com/books?id=SkAEAAAAMBAJ&printsec (PD image).*
Page 11 – Photos circa 1971, creators unknown.
Sources: reddit.com/r/OldSchoolCool/comments/890bq6/ and daemen.edu/about/give-daemen/founders-celebration-events/college-history-timeline. Pre-1978, no renewed copyright.
Page 12 – Photos unknown dates and creators. Sources: footage.framepool.com/shotimg/524716167. Pre-1978, no copyright mark (PD image) and jimmysirrelslovechild.co.uk/fans/stoke-1970. Pre-1978, no copyright mark (PD image).
Page 13 – Women's Liberation protest 8th Nov 1971.
Source: redflagwalks.wordpress.com/category/womens-liberation/. Pre-1978 (PD image).
– Boy crossing road, date and creator unknown. Pre-1978, no copyright mark (PD image).
Page 14 – From *Life* Magazine 8th Jan 1971. Source: books.google.com/books?id=nFMEAAAAMBAJ&printsec (PD image).*
Page 15 – Decimal Day posters from Woolworths and British Rail. Sources: woolworthsmuseum.co.uk/1970s-decimalisation.html and nationalarchives.gov.uk/education/resources/significant events/british-rail-goes-decimal-1971/. – Industrial Relations protest, creator unknown. Pre-1978, no copyright mark (PD image). – Engineers strike, 1973, creator unknown. All images this page pre-1978, no copyright mark (PD image).
Page 16 – Commune members, source: allthatsinteresting.com/hippie-communes.
– Commune members pose in front of a tipi, by John Olson from Life Magazine, 18th Jul 1969. Source: books.google.com/books?id=K08EAAAAMBAJ&printsec.
Page 17 – Tending to the fields, source: burlingtonfreepress.com/story/news/local/vermont/2015/07/24/vermont-remains-hippie-epicenter/30564907/, photo by Rebecca Lepkoff of Vermont Historical Society. Pre-1978. – Geodesic dome, source: vpr.org/post/communes-hippie-invasion-and-how-1970s-changed-state#stream/0 by Kate Daloz. Pre-1978.
– Commune bus, source: allthatsinteresting.com/hippie-communes. Pre-1978. (PD image).
Page 18 – From *Life* Magazine 8th Jan 1971.
Source: books.google.com/books?id=nFMEAAAAMBAJ&printsec (PD* image).
Page 19 – *All in the Family*, 4th May 1971, by CBS Television.** Source: en.wikipedia.org/wiki/All_in_the_Family#/media/File: Archie_and_Lionel_All_in_the_Family_1971.JPG.
Page 20 – Still image and poster from the TV series *Hawaii Five-O* by CBS, 1970.** – *Marcus Welby MD*. cast, source: commons.wikimedia.org/wiki/File:Marcus_Welby_MD_cast.JPG. Pre-1978 (PD image).
Page 21 – Sonny & Cher publicity image by CBS Television, 1971. Source: en.wikipedia.org/wiki/Sonny_%26_Cher#/media/ File:Sonny_and_Cher_1971.JPG. (PD image). – *The New Dick Van Dyke Show*, by CBS.** – *Columbo*, publicity photo by NBC, 31st May 1973. Source: commons.wikimedia.org/wiki/Category:People_of_the_United_States_in_1973#/media/File: Columbo_Peter_Falk_1973.JPG. (PD image). – *The Two Ronnies*, image from the *1971-1987 TV series(complete series) DVD-R*. Pre-1978 (PD image).
Page 22 – Source: flickr.com/photos/91591049@N00/25556659600/ by SenseiAlan. Attribution 4.0 Internat. (CC BY 4.0).
Page 23 – Boston Traffic in 1971, creator unknown. Source: newenglanddiary.com/home/tag/Boston+traffic. Pre-1978.
Page 24 – 1971 Dodge Demon 340 and 1971 Mercury Comet GT. Source: flickr.com/photos/91591049@N00/12363684144/ and flickr.com/photos/91591049@N00/22547999418/ by SenseiAlan. Attribution 4.0 International (CC BY 4.0). – 1971 Vega by Chevrolet from *Life* 5th March 1971.
Source: books.google.com/books?id=31MEAAAAMBAJ&printsec (PD* image).
Page 25 – 1971 Datsun 240-Z and 1971 Saab by SenseiAlan, source: flickr.com/photos/91591049@N00/48487590496/ and flickr.com/photos/91591049@N00/26342605796/. Attribution 4.0 International (CC BY 4.0). – 1971 Toyota from *Life* Magazine 5th Nov.
Source: books.google.com/books?id=FkAEAAAAMBAJ&printsec (PD* image).
Page 26 – Source: flickr.com/photos/91591049@N00/24957417155/ by SenseiAlan. Attribution 4.0 Internat. (CC BY 4.0).
Page 27 – From *Life* Magazine 1st Oct 1971.
Source: books.google.com/books?id=B0AEAAAAMBAJ& printsec (PD* image).
Page 28 – Source: latimes.com/local/california/la-me-lopez-la-better-worse-20180825-story. Pre-1978.
– Chart: epa.gov/ transportation-air-pollution-and-climate-change/accomplishments-and-success-air-pollution-transportation.
Page 29 – Sources: insider.com/vintage-photos-los-angeles-smog-pollution-epa-2020-1.
– commons.wikimedia.org/wiki/ File:Two_California_Plaza_-_350_S._Grand_Avenue,_Los_Angeles.
– commons.wikimedia.org/wiki/File:EAST_RIVER_AND_ MANHATTAN_SKYLINE_IN_HEAVY_SMOG_-_NARA_-_548365. – quora.com/What-does-the-British-phrase-it-was-a-real-pea-souper-mean.
All images pre-1978 (PD images).

Page 30 – Greenpeace founders by Robert Keziere, source: www-dev.greenpeace.org/test-uranus/about/our-history/.
Page 31 – *Operation Crossroads*, Bikini Atoll, 25th July 1946. Source: en.wikipedia.org/wiki/Operation_Crossroads. – *Small Boy* at Nevada Proving Grounds, 14th July 1962. Source: commons.wikimedia.org/wiki/File:Small_Boy_nuclear_test_1962.jpg. Photos this page by either U.S. Army or Navy. (PD images).
Page 32 – Advertisement by US Women's Army Corps. Pre-1978, no copyright mark (PD image).
Page 33 – PD images the U.S. News & World Report collection at the Library of Congress Prints and Photo division. – Jane Fonda, press conference 18th Jan 1975. Source: commons.Wikimedia.org/wiki/File:Jane_Fonda_1975c by Mieremet, Rob / Anefo. From the Dutch National Archives (PD image).
Page 35 – From *Life* Magazine 7th May 1971. Source: books.google.com/books?id=LUAEAAAAMBAJ& printsec (PD image).*
Page 36 – Apollo 14 crew, by NASA. Source: nasa.gov/image-feature/apollo-14-crew-portrait (PD image). – Apollo 15 with Rover, by NASA. Source: nasa.gov/centers/marshall/history/this-week-in-nasa-history-apollo-15-astronauts-deploy-first-lunar-roving-vehicle-july.html (PD image). – Atlas-Centaur carrying Mariner 9 by the US Air Force. Source en.wikipedia.org/wiki/Mariner_9#/media/File:Atlas_I-CENTAUR.jpg (PD image).
Page 37 – Salyut 1 by NASA/David S. F. Portree, NASA Reference Publication 1357 (March 1995) (PD image) – Soviet stamp, 1971. Source: en.wikipedia.org/wiki/Soyuz_11 (PD image).
– Mars 3 source: en.wikipedia.org/wiki/Mars_3 (PD image).
Page 38 – Salem Advert, source: ebay. Creator unknown. Pre-1978, no copyright mark (PD) image.
Page 39 – Source: pinterest.com.au/pin/333196072430850347/. Pre-1978, no mark (PD) image.
Page 40 & 41 – Republican arrests, creators unknown. Source: anphoblacht.com/contents/26282. Pre-1978, no copyright mark (PD images). – Peace Wall by Robin Kirk, 2008.
Source flickr.com/photos/rightsatduke/4595426547/. Attribution 4.0 International (CC BY 4.0).
– Bloody Sunday riots, creator unknown. Source: britainfirst.org/army_northern_ireland_veterans_stitched_up_and_sold_down_the_river. Pre-1978, no copyright mark (PD images).
Page 42 – Pakistan surrender, source: commons.wikimedia.org/wiki/Category:Bangladesh_Liberation_War (PD image).
Page 43 – From *Life* Magazine 7th May 1971.
Source books.google.com/books?id=LUAEAAAAMBAJ& printsec (PD* image).
Page 44 – Manson, by Mitch Hell. Source: flickr.com/photos/64162818@N04/6301022922. Attribution-NoDerivatives 4.0 International (CC BY-ND 4.0).
– Sharon Tate, source: commons.wikimedia.org/wiki/Category:Sharon_Tate (PD image).
Page 45 – From *Life* Magazine 6th Aug 1971.
Source books.google.com/books?id=QUAEAAAAMBAJ&printsec (PD image).*
Page 46 – Walt Disney World images, sources: disneyparks.disney.go.com/blog/2010/10/this-day-in-history-walt-disney-world-resort-officially-opens-1971/, flickr.com/photos/iainstars/19490317806/ and en.wikipedia.org/wiki/Walt_Disney_World. All images -ShareAlike 4.0 International (CC BY-SA 4.0).
Page 47 – Webber, 2006. Source: commons.wikimedia.org/wiki/Category:Andrew_Lloyd_Webber (PD image). – Production photos from *Jesus Christ Superstar* (1971)** by Friedman-Abeles, from New York Public Library Billy Rose Theatre Division. Shelf locator: *T-VIM 1992-013.
Source: digitalcollections.nypl.org/items/c6adebf8-212c-4780-e040-e00a1806321a.
Page 48 – Still images from the films *Needle Park* by 20th Century Fox** and *Carnal Knowledge* by AVCO Embassy Pictures.**
Page 49 – Film posters for the movies: *A Clockwork Orange* by Warner Bros.** , *Fiddler on the Roof* by United Artists,** and *The French Connection* by 20th Century Fox. **
Page 50 – Film posters for the movies: *The Poseidon Adventure* by 20th Century Fox,** *The Towering Inferno* by 20th Century Fox,** *Earthquake* by Universal Pictures,** and *Tidalwave* by Toho.**
Page 52 – Marvin Gaye album cover by Tamla (Motown Records) and John Lennon *Imagine* album cover by Apple Records. Images are reproduced under fair use terms for informational purposes only. No alternative free image exists. These images are of low resolution and will not devalue the ability of the creator to profit from the original works.
Page 53 – Glastonbury pyramid stage by Robert Bloomfield, 1971. Source: metro.co.uk/2011/06/23/glastonbury-festival-1971-a-blast-from-the-glast-55527/?ito=cbshare. – Celebration of Life, creator unknown. Source: stereolp.blogspot.com/2010/06/celebration-of-life-festival-june-21-28.html (PD).**
Page 54 – Rod Stuart (cropped photo) for Mercury Records in *Billboard* 6th Nov 1971.
Source: commons.wikimedia.org/ wiki/Category:Rod_Stewart. Pre-1978, no copyright mark (PD image).
– The Osmonds publicity photo for MGM Records, 28th Nov 1971. Source: commons.wikimedia.org/wiki/Category:The_Osmonds (PD image). – John Denver publicity photo for RCA records, 9th Aug 1973.
Source: commons.wikimedia.org/wiki/Category:John_Denver. Pre-1978, no copyright mark (PD image).
– The Bee Gees on *The Midnight Special*, NBC TV, 1973.
Source: commons.wikimedia.org/wiki/Category:Bee_Gees. Pre-1978, no copyright mark (PD image).
Page 55 – Tom Jones, from ABC TV *This is Tom Jones*, 10th Nov 1969. Permission PD-PRE1978. Source: commons. wikimedia.org/wiki/Category:Tom_Jones_(singer) (PD image). – The Carpenters, White House photo by Knudsen, Robert L from the National Archives, Identifier (NAID) 194770. (PD image).
Page 56 – Source: flickr.com/photos/nesster/5749980453/ by Nesster. Attribution 4.0 Int (CC BY 4.0).
Page 57 – From *Life* Magazine 4th June 1971.
Source: books.google.com/books?id=Q0EEAAAAMBAJ& printsec (PD image).*

Page 58 – Pants and skirt-suit, 1969, creator unknown. Pre-1978, (PD image). – Maxi-dress by YSL, Spring-Summer 1969. Source: minniemuse.com/articles/creative-connections/ patchwork. (PD image).
Page 59 – Elizabeth Taylor, source: instyle.com/celebrity/transformations/elizabeth-taylors-changing-looks. – Thea Porter dress, photographer Patrick Hunt, 1970. – Weipert and Burda fashion show, Apr 1972, photo by Friedrich Magnussen. Permission CC BY-SA 3.0 DE. – Mini dresses, sources: pinterest.com/pin/99782947967669796/ and retrospace.org/2011_01_01_archive.html unknown photographers. Pre-1978, no copyright mark (PD image).
Page 60 – Fashions from Sears Catalogues, pre-1978, no copyright mark (PD image). – Hungarian singer Szűcs Judit wears embroidered demin. Source: commons.wikimedia.org/wiki/File:Szűcs_Judit_énekesnő._Fortepan_88657.jpg. Licensed under the Creative Commons Attribution-Share Alike 3.0 Unported. – Dacron pants from the 1975 J.C. Penney catalog. Pre-1978, (PD image). – Flared jumpsuits, creator unknown. Pre-1978, (PD image).
Page 61 – From *Life* Magazine 7th May 1971.
Source: books.google.com/books?id=LUAEAAAAMBAJ& printsec (PD image).*
Page 62 – Nik Nik shirts, polyester jumpsuits, and knit pantsuits, source: onedio.com/haber/erkekte-retro-modasinin-tutmamasinin-32-mantikli-sebebi-300983. – Polyester tops and pants, toweling jumpsuits, and shrink tops by Colombia Minerva, source: flashbak.com/the-good-the-bad-and-the-tacky-20-fashion-trends-of-the-1970s-26213/. – Denim on denim source: typesofjeanfits.com/a-brief-history-of-jeans-denim-history-timeline/. – Safari suits source: klyker.com/ 1970s-fashion/. All images this page pre-1978, no copyright mark or renewal (PD image).
Page 63 – Still image from the film *Saturday Night Fever* by Paramount Pictures.**
Source: vocal.media/beat/the-list-saturday-night-fever-40th-anniversary. – Dancers Studio 54, sources: definition.org/studio-54/2/ &alexilubomirski.com/ image-collections/studio-54 (PD images).
Page 64 – From *Life* Magazine 3rd Dec 1971.
Source: books.google.com/books?id=HUAEAAAAMBAJ&printsec (PD* image).
Page 65 – Ali vs Frazier, promotional poster. Source: en.wikipedia.org/wiki/Joe_Frazier#/media/File:Ali_vs_frazier_ elgra fico.jpg. Pre-1978 (PD images). – Kahn, creator unknown. Source: dawn.com/news/1423231. Pre-1978, no mark (PD images). – Goolagong, 1st Aug 1971, from Nationaal Archief. Source: nationaalarchief.nl/onderzoeken/fotocollectie/ abc86f8c-d0b4-102d-bcf8-003048976d84. Pre-1978 (PD images). – King in 1973, unknown creator. Source: en.wikipedia. org/wiki/Billie_Jean_King#/media/File:Billie_Jean_King_and_Bobby_Riggs_1973.jpg. Pre-1978 (PD images).
Page 66 – From *Life* Magazine 7th May 1971.
Source: books.google.com/books?id=LUAEAAAAMBAJ&printsec. (PD* image).
Page 67 – Computers at BBN Technologies. Source: en.wikipedia.org/wiki/History_of_email#/media/File:Timesharing_and_ Development_KA-10s_at_BBN,_circa_1970.jpg (PD image). – Tomlinson, source: en.wikipedia.org/wiki/Ray_Tomlinson#/ media/File:Ray_Tomlinson_(cropped).jpg. Attribution-ShareAlike 3.0 Unported (CC BY-SA 3.0).
Page 68 – San Fernando collapsed highway by Reuben Kachadoorian, USGS, for the US Dept of the Interior. Source: commons.wikimedia.org/wiki/File:1971_San_Fernando_highway_overpass_collapse.jpg. Govt photo (PD image). – Mt Etna, creator unknown. Source: italysvolcanoes.com/gifs/image/1971StuBW_01.jpg. Pre-1978, (PD image). – Golden Gate Bridge by Matt Faluotico. Source: commons.wikimedia.org/wiki/Category:Golden_Gate_Bridge#/media/File:Almost_ Baker_Beach _(135919049).jpeg licensed under Creative Commons Attribution 3.0 Unported.
Page 69 – Kennedy Center, unknown photographer. Source: commons.wikimedia.org/wiki/File:KennedyCenterFromAir2. JPG (PD image). – Neruda by Annemarie Heinrich, 1967. Source: commons.wikimedia.org/wiki/Category:Portraits_of_Pablo_Neruda#/media/File:Pablo_Neruda_by_Annemarie_Heinrich,_1967.jpg. (PD image).
Page 70 – 1971 Print magazine advertisement for the Peace Corps (PD image).*
Page 71 – 1971 Print magazine advertisement for United Van Lines (PD image).*
Page 72-74 – All photos are, where possible, CC BY 2.0 or PD images made available by the creator for free use including commercial use. Where commercial use images are unavailable, photos are included here for information only under U.S. fair use laws due to: 1- images are low resolution copies; 2- images do not devalue the ability of the copyright holders to profit from the original works in any way; 3- Images are too small to be used to make illegal copies for use in another book; 4- The images are relevant to the article created.
Page 75 – From *Life* Magazine 2nd July 1971.
Source: books.google.com/books?id=OUAEAAAAMBAJ& printsec (PD image).*
Page 78 – 1971 Print magazine advertisement for Hellmann's Mayonnaise (PD image).*
Page 79 – 1971 Print magazine advertisement for the Keep America Beautiful campaign (PD image).*

*Advertisement (or image from an advertisement) is in the public domain because it was published in a collective work (such as a periodical issue) in the US between 1925 and 1977 and without a copyright notice specific to the advertisement.
**Posters for movies or events are either in the public domain (published in the US between 1925 and 1977 and without a copyright notice specific to the artwork) or owned by the production company, creator, or distributor of the movie or event. Posters, where not in the public domain, and screen stills from movies or TV shows, are reproduced here under USA Fair Use laws due to: 1- images are low resolution copies; 2- images do not devalue the ability of the copyright holders to profit from the original works in any way; 3- Images are too small to be used to make illegal copies for use in another book; 4- The images are relevant to the article created.

This book was written by Bernard Bradforsand-Tyler as part of *A Time Traveler's Guide* series of books.

All rights reserved. The author exerts the moral right to be identified as the author of the work.

No parts of this book may be reproduced, stored in any retrieval system, or transmitted in any form or by any means, without prior written permission from the author.

This is a work of nonfiction. No names have been changed, no events have been fabricated. The content of this book is provided as a source of information for the reader, however it is not meant as a substitute for direct expert opinion. Although the author has made every effort to ensure that the information in this book is correct at time of printing, and while this publication is designed to provide accurate information in regard to the subject matters covered, the author assumes no responsibility for errors, inaccuracies, omissions, or any other inconsistencies herein and hereby disclaims any liability to any party for any loss, damage, or disruption caused by errors or omissions.

All images contained herein are reproduced with the following permissions:
- Images included in the public domain.
- Images obtained under creative commons license.
- Images included under fair use terms.
- Images reproduced with owner's permission.

All image attributions and source credits are provided at the back of the book. All images are the property of their respective owners and are protected under international copyright laws.

First printed in 2020 in the USA (ISBN 978-0-6450623-9-7).
Revised in 2024, 2nd Edition (978-1-922676-24-5).
Self-published by B. Bradforsand-Tyler.

www.ingramcontent.com/pod-product-compliance
Lightning Source LLC
Chambersburg PA
CBHW072105110526
44590CB00018B/3317